What readers and the media in Alabama say about previous books by John M. Wood:

"(*The Successful Divorce*)... has good advice for those divorcing in Alabama."

Birmingham News

"*Saving Your Assets* is the most practical and clearly written book on the subject of money and divorce in Alabama. To keep the assets you have, read this book."

Jeff Hammock
Private Investigator

"In his book, (John) Wood outlines the important steps to take when a woman has made the decision to end her marriage...."

Baptist Health System publication

"Wood hits hard because, he says, your divorce decisions will affect the rest of your life and your children's lives. If you agree to things you don't understand...you'll deal with the consequences for years."

Anniston TimesDaily

"I have already received more information from this book than I have from my lawyer during the entire case. This should be required reading for anyone who is going through a divorce."

Maggie from Mobile
Amazon.com

MORE SUCCESSFUL DIVORCE IN ALABAMA

John M. Wood

Published by PSG Books
Dallas, Texas

More Successful Divorce in Alabama

Published by PSG Books
An imprint of Professional Solutions Group
9603 White Rock Trail, Suite 310
Dallas, Texas 75238
214/340-6223
214/340-6209 fax
acquisitions@psgbooks.com

Books published under the PSG Books imprint are distributed to the U.S. book trade by Independent Publishers Group, 814 N. Franklin St., Chicago, Illinois 60610, 1-(800)-888-4741. Resellers outside the book trade who wish to purchase books in quantity at a discount may contact PSG Books toll free at 1-(800)-465-1508.

ISBN 0-9659273-8-5

Manufactured in the United States of America

9 8 7 6 5 4 3 2 1

John M. Wood, Author and Attorney, is available to speak to groups throughout Alabama and the South on divorce, the financial aspects of marital dissolution, child custody and related subjects. He can be reached at the John M. Wood Family Law Center, 3020 Pumphouse Road, Birmingham, Alabama 35243, (205) 970-4142, john@woodfamilylaw.com.

Library of Congress Cataloging-in-Publication Data

Wood, John M., atty at law.
More successful divorce in Alabama / John M. Wood.
p. cm.
Summary: "Designed to help Alabama residents survive divorce according to the laws of their state with the help of an attorney. Is not a how-to book for people handling their own divorces"--Provided by publisher.
ISBN 0-9659273-8-5
1. Divorce--Law and legislation--Alabama--Popular works. I. Title.
KFA100.Z9W65 2005
346.76101'66--dc22

2004025275

NOTICE

State laws and legal precedents vary greatly and change over time, so the reader should not use this book for specific legal advice. Every divorce case and post-divorce action is unique, requiring the advice of those versed in the laws of the jurisdiction where the action is taken.

It must be understood, therefore, that this book will provide readers only with a general overview of the divorce process and post-divorce issues, so that they may be better informed and can decide whether to take legal action or otherwise address these issues.

This book is not intended to provide legal advice. Consult an attorney for specific information related to your personal situation.

Table of Contents

PART TWO

The Heart of the Case

PART THREE

What Happens After the Divorce

Acknowledgments

Success — to laugh often and much; to win the respect of intelligent people and the affection of children; to know even one life has breathed easier because you have lived … this is to have succeeded.

Ralph Waldo Emerson

Having endured my parents' divorce as a child, I feel uniquely qualified to describe the pain of divorce and the struggle to overcome it. My parents' divorce gave me tremendous insight into my priorities in life. Until my mother's death, she and I shared a bond that allowed us to overcome the obstacles inherent in an ugly divorce. I am thankful for the time spent with my wonderful mother, sister and brother. I am still close to my siblings, in part, because of the struggles of the past. The confidence and security I received from them allowed me to write *The Successful Divorce* and this updated edition as well as co-author *Saving Your Assets When You Can't Save Your Marriage.*

My intense focus on family problems is a direct result of the experiences I encountered as a young child. If anything positive came out of that terrible situation, it is the understanding of my primary goal. In practicing divorce and custody law, I want to help my clients successfully maneuver through situations that other people have been forced to endure alone.

From the bottom of my heart, I thank all of my clients for allowing me the opportunity to help them, and now you. I hope this book will help you avoid the heartache I have witnessed others endure.

John M. Wood

About the Author

John M. Wood is head of the John M. Wood Family Law Center in Birmingham, Alabama. This firm is devoted exclusively to matrimonial law, including child custody and divorce litigation. John left a successful tenure with one of the state's largest firms because of a desire to develop a practice concentrating in divorce and custody issues.

As a child of divorce himself, John is keenly aware that domestic problems often present clients with the most important legal issues they will ever face.

His goal in writing *The Successful Divorce* back in the late 1990s was to educate clients that decisions related to divorce must be thoroughly thought out, because they will have long-lasting consequences. The effect of divorce lasts throughout the lifetimes of the parties, including not only the husband and wife, but the children and other family members as well. These effects have not changed over time, but some trends in the law have changed. *More Successful Divorce in Alabama* is a complete revision of the first book. It addresses changes in the laws of the state as well as updating differing societal trends that relate to divorce and family.

John is also co-author of *Saving Your Assets When You Can't Save Your Marriage*. This book on the financial aspects of divorce was released in 2002 and is available in bookstores and online at Amazon.com.

John realizes that divorce does not solve every problem. Indeed, decisions made during a divorce will often impact entire families and create new situations and challenges for everyone. He is an active member of Liberty Park Baptist Church, where he is heavily involved in mission work in third-world countries. He also supports numerous charitable organizations, including The Big Oak Ranch home for children.

He graduated from the prestigious Georgetown University Law School and is a member of the American Bar Association, Alabama Bar Association and the Birmingham Bar Association. He served as chairman and treasurer of the Family Law Section of the Alabama State Bar Association and on the Fee Arbitration Committee of the Birmingham Bar Association.

John has been honored by the Birmingham Business Journal as one of the city's *Top 40 Under 40*, recognizing young leaders in the business and civic arena.

Publisher

Introduction

There is some good news about divorce in Alabama. Since I wrote my original book, *The Successful Divorce*, in 1997, the rate of divorce has declined. In 1990, there were 6.1 divorces per 1,000 people. By 2001, that rate decreased to 5.3 per thousand. Several important features of Alabama life contributed to the lessening rate; the unprecedented economic prosperity of the 90s, increases in the age at which people marry in the state and heightened interest by churches and government in premarital education.

Divorce is a twentieth century phenomenon. Since World War II, when women were forced to work in the factories and discovered they could care for themselves, the number of divorces has steadily grown. With the adoption of no-fault divorce statutes by most states in the 1960s and 70s, divorce became easier and more accepted.

Our concept of successful divorce runs counter to prevailing thought, since it describes an intelligent approach to an insane process. Each divorce is unique, and the various facts, assets, debts and faults of each individual marriage will be considered in the resolution of the divorce. Anyone who blindly enters into the divorce arena must understand that the consequences of your actions will follow you throughout your life. But divorce doesn't have to be the end. On the contrary, a successful divorce is one you move into with knowledge and foresight, protecting yourself and the ones you love. If the process works as it should, you have not lost your shirt, but instead you have your life back and your children are emotionally intact.

The entire process of divorce oftentimes is compared to jungle warfare. For each spouse, the pathway is dark and unfamiliar territory, much like a jungle. The process often feels like warfare, where each side plans skirmishes and court battles before the ultimate resolution of the case.

Many people believe the government should make divorce more difficult. Several states have attempted to repeal the statutes that make divorce easily obtainable, while others are trying to make it more difficult to get married in the first place. Finally, the curve on the graph of divorce has turned sideways, but still the battle lines are drawn.

This book makes numerous references to the husband and the wife, as well as referencing "she" and "he," the "parents" and the "parties." It should be apparent from the context that I am talking about the people who are divorcing. This material is intended to be applicable to both the husband and the wife. For purposes of this book, please accept the "he/she" references as being applicable to both parties and not any kind of gender-based designation, including references to "the attorney." There are many excellent male and female matrimonial lawyers, and all references apply to both.

The examples used in this book are loosely based on prior cases. Most examples are composites of people and situations I have become familiar with in the Alabama court system. No references should be construed to indicate that only a wife or only a husband could act in a particular manner. Plenty of husbands and wives act equally horribly, both during the marriage and while going through a divorce. In fact, one of the most critical questions I can ask during an initial interview is, "Now that you have told me how terrible your spouse is, what is he (or she) going to say about you?" As they say, Snow White doesn't marry Hitler. Few people are so outrageously awful that they are 100% responsible for a breakup or so perfect that they are without fault. You can only help your attorney by telling the unvarnished truth, no matter how embarrassing that might be.

Women have affairs and men have affairs, women take drugs and men take drugs, women lie and men lie. In fact, one well-known domestic judge once said after a heated trial that since the parties told such different stories and both parties had sworn under oath that they were telling the truth, they could not have been married to each other. In many cases, each party will claim the other side is lying. You need to realize that your spouse may lie to ensure a favorable result. If this type of behavior is expected, get ready for it, so it won't disrupt your case.

This book is primarily based on the statutes and currently controlling case law for the state of Alabama, since that is where I practice. If you live in another state, though, the key concepts in this material are still worth reading to familiarize you with the divorce process. For example, you will need to hire an attorney and prepare for trial. I have attempted to make this material serve as a guide to preparing for your divorce, regardless of where you live. But this is not a how-to book. Reading this book does not prepare you to represent yourself in a divorce. There are times when people can represent themselves. We talk about those times in a chapter on hiring your attorney. If your divorce is truly uncontested, you may not need an attorney. However, I strongly recommend that you seek counsel. Usually the divorce process is too complicated even for the attorney who is not a matrimonial specialist, let alone non-lawyers.

Because the legal situations cited here are based on Alabama law, you need to consult an attorney in your state to determine the specific applicability of any particular provisions.

More Successful Divorce in Alabama addresses the divorce process and its various stages, from the selection of an attorney through settlement or trial, to the difficulty of enforcing your divorce decree, to post-divorce actions. Along the way, issues ranging from child custody to property division are discussed. This material serves as an overview of the major issues surrounding a divorce, and each case hinges on its own facts. This book is not a replacement for specific legal advice or independent counsel.

John M. Wood

PART 1

Pretrial: Readying Yourself For the Storm

Don't go to divorce court for justice.
Go simply for a conclusion.

Anonymous divorce lawyer

CHAPTER ONE

In a Perfect World, There Would Be No Divorce Attorneys

WE LIVE IN THE ERA of disposable relationships. Everywhere we look, people are shedding themselves of their mates. The 1970s were the most prolific years for divorce. Across the country, about 65% of all marriages failed during that time period. People were dumping their mates for subtle reasons such as "we've grown apart." Divorce had a profound effect on children who are now old enough to marry. Their rates of marriage are at all-time lows as the divorce rate has flattened out to about 43%.

Someone once said that we treat our spouses like we do our socks, discarding them after light use. Only we're much nicer to the socks, since we don't actually throw them out but simply toss them where they won't be in the way. To continue the analogy, an increasing number of us are going bare-footed, choosing not to commit to any particular pair of socks. Alabama has one of the lowest rates of people living together without being married, but even here the number of cohabitating couples is staggering.

There's Too Much Divorce

No matter how many people marry and divorce in Alabama these days, the process of dissolving families has taken a devastating toll. Adults become alienated from each other and their children, and many of those children never fully recover. Divorce's ripple effect on the social fabric of our society can be seen in problems relating to our schools, the incidence of crime, teen pregnancy and other unpleasant facts of life. Social science researchers disagree about the long-term effects of divorce on a nation of adult survivors of their own parents' marital problems, but you can be assured that none of them feel divorce is a good thing.

Because of the detrimental effects of divorce, I would encourage anyone to avoid it if possible. Anyone contemplating such a move should make use of every resource—marital or individual therapy, substance abuse counseling, the words of a pastor or the guidance of a close friend or advisor—to avoid the breakup of the marriage. In a perfect world, resources like these would keep more marriages together, and I would practice in another area of the law. But this isn't a perfect world, and many marriages cannot be salvaged. If all efforts to save a marriage have been exhausted and divorce is inevitable, you should work toward what we call a successful divorce, one handled with diligence and care.

Myth of the "Kind" Spouse

When divorce becomes unavoidable, most of us hope that we will continue to love and respect each other, and that we will conduct ourselves in a kind and understanding manner. But kindness can be in short supply during a divorce. Much to your dismay, you may find that a "kind" spouse can take advantage of you, fight to obtain custody of your children and do whatever is necessary to acquire your most valuable assets. For this reason, you must recognize that what happens to you in a divorce depends on your own actions. The person on the other side of the divorce may seem to be far ahead of you in thought about the situation. You must take every opportunity to protect yourself.

Initially, you may refuse to believe your soon-to-be ex might fight you at every turn, or that the person you shared your life with would refuse to do what you believe in your heart is right. You may be in for a terrible shock when your family's former breadwinner refuses to pay child support or fights for custody of the children. You may refuse to believe that your kind and loving soon-to-be ex is having an affair or is hiding assets. The shock can transform into rage when you discover this information after you've executed a settlement agreement on terms that might not have been agreeable to you if you had just known.

As a divorce attorney, I deal with a lot of family heartache. When I work to reach a settlement, my ultimate goal is to resolve the divorce with the least amount of disruption possible, especially when young children are involved. However, both parties must be willing to settle. If one party is willing to settle the case, and the other party refuses to accept the fact that a spouse is entitled to a fair distribution of the assets under the divorce, settlement is unlikely. At that point, you may be entering into a war zone and you must ready yourself for a battle of wills that may seem unnecessary but will happen nonetheless. To effectively wage that battle, you must have a lawyer who is capable and willing to aggressively litigate on your behalf. Without the willingness to push through the court system, you probably will not be able to settle.

I remember one man who refused to accept that his wife of more than 20 years was entitled even to her clothes, since they were in what he considered his house. Never mind that they both worked to pay for the house and the wife's name was on the deed. The divorce was her idea, so he felt she should just leave. He thought he was generous, allowing her to escape with the clothes on her back. In a case like this, settlement is often impossible. This kind of inflexible attitude hurts both parties. The woman was dismayed that she had to fight so hard for what rightfully was hers. No matter how much punishment the man inflicted on his long-time mate, in the end he was convinced that she had taken advantage of him.

The Battle Keeps Raging

If your spouse is obstinate during the divorce, this behavior doesn't usually end when the judge drops his gavel. Many cases result in post-divorce litigation, either dealing with the custody of children or the handling of property that remains in the names of both parties. Changes in the access of parents to their children can be especially sticky, and one party may decide to block the renovation or sale of property merely to anger the other.

If you are contemplating a divorce, are already in the middle of one, or would like to make changes to a divorce that's already granted, recognize this may be a disaster in the making. You need to get sound advice on every decision, and you want that advice from an expert. Your family and friends are not experts in divorce. Dr. Phil may have advised attorneys in the past, but he is not an attorney and is not knowledgeable about the laws that govern your marriage and divorce.

Someone needs to inform you that for purposes of this action alone, your spouse is now the enemy. You are entering a battlefield called the legal system and are about to go to war. If the war starts, you need to be ready, know the rules and prepare to face the consequences of battle.

May your last decision as a married couple be your best decision as a married couple.

An Alabama Circuit Court Judge

CHAPTER TWO

How An Awful Divorce Can Make A Bad Marriage Even Worse

WE SHOULD APPROACH DIVORCE the way we did as a child, when a bully punched us in the stomach. Both actions are devastating and take your breath away. Rage headlong after the bully and you will probably get hurt even worse. It makes more sense to sit down, catch your breath and carefully consider your response.

Before proceeding with a divorce action, you should exhaust every avenue available to save the marriage. Seek help from your pastor, marriage counselors and support groups. Talk with co-workers, family members and friends. If you have children, talk to parents who've done exactly what you are now contemplating. See how it affected them and their children, and how you can get through it safely. Gather information, but don't reveal too much of yourself. Any one of these people could be called by the other side to testify against you at trial. They may have no other choice than to tell the truth about you on the witness stand.

"In my experience, many people jump into the idea of divorce as a way of trying to find relief for their emotional pain," says Bart Grooms, M.Div., M.Ed., of the Samaritan Counseling Center of Baptist Health System in Birmingham. "I try to show couples that most people can find healing for their pain by making changes in the relationship, and that they and their children stand to gain enormously.

"Divorce will always be an option for people who simply cannot improve things no matter how hard they work at it. But that should be a last resort. It's amazing how many people stop thinking about divorce once they realize that constructive change is possible."

Divorce Creates A New Set of Problems

Divorce is not a quick fix for marital problems. It is an emotionally draining process which creates a set of problems different from those you encountered during the marriage. A good attorney should make every effort to ensure that you are prepared for the process and aware of opportunities to save your relationship.

At the same time, you may be caught in the middle of an abusive or violent situation that could escalate into tragedy. In an abusive or controlling situation, a decision must be made immediately, for your safety and the safety of your children. Once that decision has been made, you must get sound legal advice and utilize the police and court system to prevent further abuse.

Realize that even though you are divorcing, you may still have considerable contact with your former spouse. If there are no children involved, you may never have to deal with your spouse after the divorce. If you do have children, usually you will communicate regularly with your former spouse concerning the care of the children. Both parents have legal rights related to the children, and are normally afforded certain protections by the court. Consider what the relationship will be between the parties after the divorce.

You may be surprised how difficult it is to raise children in two separate homes. Daily responsibilities are greatly magnified with only one person doing them. You may have total responsibility for thousands of lunches, carpools and practice sessions or sporting events. You may have to make last-minute decisions when you have a sick child and have to go to work. And you may constantly worry about the lack of good parental influences.

Even in marriages where one parent is the primary caretaker for the children, the other spouse usually serves as a backup caretaker in an emergency. At the same time, life can be peaceful without a difficult spouse. All of this is part of creating the successful divorce. Even though I regret seeing people split up their families, it can be thrilling to see my clients rediscover themselves after they get away from controlling or abusive spouses. The decision to divorce must be made on an individual basis, but it can only be made after assessing all the present and future issues you know or can imagine.

Listen to "Experts" At Your Peril

"I just saw a show on Oprah about custody and this is what she said I need to do," a former client began. Many clients begin their research into their rights this way. A long line of co-workers, friends and family members will offer you plenty of advice if you decide to divorce. Talk shows will lure you with topics like "Leaving your Husband" or "The Mistakes You Can Make in

Your Divorce." Magazine articles on failing relationships and the divorce process will call out to you from newsstands. None of these sources know all the secrets of your marriage, though, and no one can give you accurate advice without all of the facts. This information is based on a limited experience with situations that are distinctly different from yours. You will hear that women always get more than 50% of the assets, and that fathers never get custody of the kids. As a result, these war stories can skew your idea of what is possible. Inevitably, they will damage your pursuit of a successful divorce.

The time to seek help from family and friends is before you decide the divorce is inevitable. After the decision is made, you should lean on family and friends for emotional support, but turn to an expert for legal advice. Many people are reluctant to ask for advice about marital problems because they are embarrassed or ashamed. But a lack of knowledge of issues related to divorce can result in grossly misguided decisions.

Hire As Much Expertise in Family Law As You Need

An amazing number of people fail to get legal advice until after they feel cheated in their divorce. People who don't have a problem paying whatever it costs for an expert to repair a car will save money by turning to a family member, friend or a TV expert for a legal opinion when it comes to divorce. Often people will consult an attorney who knows little or nothing about divorce law. Granted, some situations are simple enough to be handled by a legal generalist. But when you are dealing with your children's lives and your financial future, you are rolling the dice and potentially making the wrong decision to venture through the minefield with novice help. This is not a gamble you should be willing to take.

If you are unhappy with the outcome of your divorce, the court will not give you special consideration because you thought your spouse would be fair. If you had an opportunity to obtain expert legal advice, and chose not to because you did not know any better or did not want to pay for it, the court is not likely to change the agreement you made. If you do not properly handle your divorce action the first time, the adage that "you made your bed, you have to lie in it" will become hauntingly true in a post-divorce action.

Post-Divorce Actions Are Expensive

Making things right the first time is an essential element of a successful divorce. You are able to amend a problem by filing an appeal or asking to modify your divorce decree. But you will often spend more money on a post-divorce action than you would if you had fixed the problem at the start. And money is only one element. I cannot begin to describe the emotion that clients display when they realize that they gave up custody of their children in the divorce and may not be able to change custody now.

One naïve young woman came to our office soon after her divorce was final. She wanted custody of her little girl but mistakenly gave her husband custody in the divorce agreement. The husband told the wife that he did not want custody, but that the papers had to say he got custody for the judge to approve the agreement because the wife had not been in her apartment long enough. The young wife was not represented by counsel in the original matter, but she signed the divorce agreement of her own free will. She genuinely believed she was going to get custody because her husband told her so.

Within days after executing the agreement, the wife found out that the husband had been having an affair and that he was not going to allow her to keep the child because "the papers said that he got custody."

We were able to reverse the outcome of that case, but the wife incurred a tremendous financial and emotional expense to ultimately get her child back. In most cases like this one, people create an unfixable mess because they did not hire an expert in the beginning. There is a plumbing company in Birmingham that uses the clever slogan, "We Repair What Your Husband Fixed." In divorce law, this could be adapted to "We Fix The Settlement You Accepted." Many times, though, in dealing with serious matters of custody, parents are forced to accept that they have lost their children due to their own bad decision making.

It's difficult to tell which gives some
couples the most happiness,
the minister who marries them,
or the judge who divorces them.

Mary Wilson Little, from "I Do to I'll Sue"

CHAPTER THREE

Working Toward An Uncontested Divorce

WE SHOULD ALL HOPE that if divorce becomes necessary, matters can be worked out so that the dissolution is amicable and, therefore, uncontested. The divorce may happen grudgingly, and certainly there is always resentment. But a divorce without contest is possible. It only happens when two people, who no longer see eye-to-eye on anything, agree on every issue related to the dissolution of their marriage. It doesn't happen too often.

If one spouse does exactly what the other spouse wants, an uncontested divorce will happen every time. But when you combine the parties' egos, pride, jealousy, rage and resentment with the resolution of custody and property issues, it is difficult to forge an agreement. We talk to people everyday who want to know the fee for an uncontested divorce, because they have an agreement and "all we need is for a lawyer to prepare the papers."

When we ask whether the other party agrees with the terms of the divorce, the usual response is "No, but it's what I want and I'm sure that I can make it happen." A situation like this will often become contested. Even when the client says the other spouse is in total agreement, we rarely believe it until the documents are signed and filed with the court.

Restrain Yourself

Many solid agreements fall apart because one spouse gets in a horrible fight with the other before the papers are executed. For that reason alone, clients should watch what they say until the divorce is final. Emotions run high during the resolution of a divorce. One party may say something awful to the other spouse and a simple uncontested divorce becomes contested out of nothing more than pride and anger.

In an uncontested divorce, sometimes the parties opt to use only one attorney. However, an attorney can legally represent only one party in the divorce and cannot advise the other party of the legal consequences of any decisions made. The attorney is looking out for the best interests of one client, and the other party's rights could be grossly affected by the terms of the agreement. Using only one attorney is not a wise move. But if it happens in your divorce, make sure you are the spouse with the attorney. Otherwise, prepare yourself for a potential disaster that can affect the rest of your life.

File the Necessary Documents

In a real sense, all divorces begin with contested issues. Think about it. Without some kind of disagreement, the parties would not be getting a divorce. In some cases, all of the issues are resolved early. Couples can obtain an uncontested divorce by having a lawyer draft the necessary pleadings and documents required by the court. Under this scenario, the party filing for divorce is called the plaintiff, and the opposing party is called the defendant on all of the court papers. The lawyer will file all executed documents with the court and the parties may be able to avoid appearing in court. These documents include the following:

Complaint: This is the first document filed in a divorce. It contains certain factual information related to the parties involved, as well as the grounds for the divorce. Generally an uncontested divorce is obtained on the basis of incompatibility, that the parties have different interests and have grown apart, and that such incompatibility cannot be reconciled.

Answer and Waiver: This document, which is typically filed second, is executed by the opposing party and answers the specific allegations contained in the complaint. It also waives any other notice requirements so the divorce can be filed and the process completed without additional delays.

Acknowledgment of Representation: This document is executed by the opposing party and states that he or she is aware that the attorney involved represents the other party, and that he or she has had an opportunity to consult with or obtain other counsel.

Testimony: This document is executed by the plaintiff, and consists of a sworn statement of the grounds for the divorce, so that the parties are not required to be present in court prior to the divorce being granted.

Settlement Agreement: The most critical document of the divorce, the settlement agreement specifies the agreement reached between the parties. Anything claimed by a party to the divorce but not addressed in this document is not usually binding on the parties and could result in conflict in the future.

Final Judgment of Divorce: Executed by the trial court judge, this document grants the divorce, approves the settlement agreement and makes it binding on both parties.

Once the parties have signed all of the documents, they are filed with the court and the judge executes the final judgment of divorce. In 1997, the Alabama legislature began to require a 30-day waiting period after the complaint is filed before a divorce can be granted. The goal of this provision is to ensure that parties have not proceeded too quickly in obtaining the divorce, and to provide an additional opportunity for reconciliation.

On the other hand, this 30-day period also can result in one party or the other attempting to repudiate the agreement and contest the divorce. Sometimes, parties have a disagreement during the waiting period. Of course, once an agreement is filed with the court, it is extremely difficult, if not impossible, to change it without filing a separate action to modify the decree.

If all the documents have been prepared properly, the parties are not usually required to appear in court and the judge will sign the divorce decree within several days or weeks.

Every divorce sinks to the level of the most irrational party.

Melvin Belli

CHAPTER FOUR

The Contested Divorce: When Rational People Fail to Agree

A CONTESTED DIVORCE is any divorce in which the parties cannot agree on the terms of the settlement. It can involve the parties and their lawyers attempting to negotiate an out-of-court settlement, or it can involve a full-blown litigated divorce in which a lawsuit is filed and tried in a courtroom.

If a divorce is being negotiated, the attorneys generally attempt to resolve the matter without a trial. Typically, a lawsuit is filed by one of the parties, and discovery and settlement negotiations are conducted while the parties anticipate a trial date.

Treat Your Spouse Like the Enemy

To get ready for a contested divorce, remember that your spouse is no longer a loyal friend who is looking out for your welfare. At least for the time being, he or she is the enemy who is trying to restrict access to your children or prevent you from receiving some material asset you believe you deserve. One of the biggest mistakes you can make in a divorce is thinking your spouse will give you what you want if you just ask. Generally, when you are this mistaken, the opposing spouse is only nice as he or she leaves the courtroom with custody of the children or all the marital assets.

Don't get me wrong. A divorce does not have to be ugly from the beginning. But a sense of realism at this time of your life is essential to the successful divorce. Friends, family and former love interests may say bad things about you out of bitterness. They may say things that are not true. What they say may be factual, but there is a good reason for your behavior. No one else may understand why you want out of a marriage. Or on the other hand, they may wonder why you wish to fight so hard to stay with a person who treats you so badly. All of this is part of the alienation and distrust inherent in the divorce process, and you should be prepared for that.

Plan Your Divorce Strategy

From a strategic point of view, all contested divorces should be handled as though they were headed to trial. If settlement efforts are successful and you wind up not going to court, you are miles ahead of the game. If settlement efforts fail, you are prepared for the worst. Fair settlements happen when you obtain adequate information at the start of your case. However, you might not even know about all of the marital assets. You may be relying on your spouse's valuation and how those assets should be divided. If your spouse has not disclosed all of the assets or is keeping other secrets, you may be agreeing to the settlement uninformed.

Unless you can prove that your spouse has hidden assets or otherwise defrauded you, the court usually will not change the agreement after the divorce has been granted.

A few years ago, a dear friend of mine gave her husband custody of their child out of fear that the divorce would become contested and the child would have to go through a bitter divorce. She did not hire a lawyer because she thought the husband would play fair with her if she did the same with him. But the husband had been abusive during the marriage. And once the divorce was granted, the wife found that her husband had been having an affair with her best friend. With facts like these, she could have won custody of her child without much of a fight. Due to the wife's naive mistake, the husband now has custody of the child and my friend sees her child on a limited basis. The wife now agonizes every day over her bad decision, and her former husband constantly reminds her that he has control over the situation.

This client asked me specifically to tell her story in this book, in the hope that someone else might not make the same tragic mistake. If she had fought for custody of her child, the emotional trauma she is now experiencing would be in the past. She took her one bite at the apple and missed. If you foolishly accept whatever settlement your spouse offers without adequate information or advice, you are dealing from a position of weakness — and weakness has never culminated in a successful divorce.

I don't believe man is woman's natural enemy. Perhaps his lawyer is.

Shana Alexander

CHAPTER FIVE

Hiring Mr. Or Ms. Right

FINDING A LAWYER IS NOT DIFFICULT. There are nearly one million attorneys in the United States and more than 11,000 licensed in Alabama alone. But connecting with a talented expert — one who makes you feel he or she can safeguard your future — can be a confusing process. The first requirement is to find a lawyer who concentrates his or her practice in matrimonial law. If your divorce is going to be contested, you want an attorney who not only knows the law, but what each individual judge prefers and looks at in each case. We use the analogy that no one wants an eye doctor to perform heart surgery. When it comes to the medical profession, people are quick to demand a specialist. Divorcing people sometimes hire just any attorney, whose specialty might be in bankruptcy or estate planning or litigating traffic tickets. Marriages that have lasted more than one year, with children or complex property arrangements, demand the services of a family law expert.

Being Your Own Lawyer

It stands to reason that if you wouldn't hire a bankruptcy lawyer to handle your divorce, you might want to think long and hard before representing yourself in family court. Fundamental to our legal system is the right to represent yourself pro se, which in Latin means "on your own behalf." More and more people are handling their own divorces, but this is no way to reach a successful divorce. Do-it-yourselfers usually take this route to save money. They believe their honest handling of divorce in a timely and rational manner makes up for their lack of knowledge, but self-service divorce lawyering can cause logjams at the courthouse and leave many litigants unsatisfied with the results.

Judges and court clerks say that people representing themselves don't know how to fill out the correct forms or what to do with them when they are filled out. They don't know how to ask questions or present evidence in court. In fact, many don't know they need evidence. All in all, it's a huge gamble you may not want to take, especially if there are children involved, larger amounts of property or a spouse who cannot be located. People often start out pro se but decide to hire an attorney after they begin the process. Or they rely on judges to instruct them, and teaching parties how to succeed is not the job of a judge.

Uncover the Correct Attorney For You

One of the best ways to begin your lawyer search is to ask some of the divorced people you know who they used and whether they were pleased with the result. If you know an attorney who practices in a field other than matrimonial law, ask him or her for recommendations. The local bar association may also have a referral service categorizing various attorneys by their specialties. In addition to these resources, clergy, counselors, accountants, financial planners and other professionals can often point you in the right direction.

Once you have the names of several attorneys, schedule initial interviews with one or more of them. When you call an attorney's office, determine the cost of this initial consultation. Divorce lawyers generally charge by the hour, and you may or may not have to pay a consultation fee for this first meeting. At the initial meeting, the attorney will want to cover the basic history of the marriage and the issues involved in the divorce. You should be as candid as possible. You may not believe it at this moment, but your spouse will not hesitate to bring up certain touchy issues such as adultery, physical abuse, substance abuse or certain sexual practices, when you try to take his or her children or a valued marital asset. The lawyer is ethically bound not to disclose the information you provide without your consent. But he or she cannot give you an honest evaluation of your case if you are not completely honest regarding the issues involved in the marriage and why you are getting a divorce. If you deal with an expert in matrimonial law, the facts of your case will not shock him or her.

A lawyer will initially determine the basic issues likely to be contested, and summarize the major assets and debts of the parties. You can assist the lawyer by providing detailed lists of all debts and assets of the marriage. In addition, the lawyer may request a narrative summarizing the reasons you want this divorce.

These interviews should also serve to educate you, especially if you are paying for them. You'll want to hear about the types of family law cases each attorney has handled. If a family business or some other valuable marital asset is at stake, you'll want to know the attorney's track record handling complex property arrangements and the resources (accountants, business valuators and appraisers) he can call upon in such cases. If children are involved, you may want to speak with clients who've been through a custody case with this attorney. And most of all, you'll want to determine if the chemistry is there between attorney and client.

You may begin your search thinking you want an attorney with the reputation as the meanest "junk yard dog" in town. But meanness often translate into obstructionism, which usually costs money, and in the long run may not lead you to a successful divorce. Some cases demand a tough-guy strategy, especially if the other side employs it. But you may decide that an attorney who can successfully settle a case without destroying the other side is more to your liking. Matching the attorney to the type of case is essential, for this person will know your deepest, darkest secrets, and you will have to work together throughout the process.

At the conclusion of the initial meeting, both you and the attorney will determine whether to proceed further. If so, the lawyer will give you homework — a list of additional information required to prepare the case — and may ask you to sign an agreement concerning legal fees.

Monitor the Cost of the Divorce

Keeping track of legal fees is an important part of the successful divorce. Most matrimonial law experts charge on an hourly basis for work performed by the lawyer and his staff. In rare cases, a flat fee rather than an hourly fee may be charged for certain limited services. A contested divorce can take a significant amount of time to bring to a successful conclusion. Each time you meet with the lawyer, he works on your case, his staff works on your case or you speak with him on the telephone, the clock is ticking. Additional time and money will be used up if he is working on an hourly basis.

Don't use your attorney as a sounding board for all the "he said, she said" gripes that are common in a contested divorce. Gossiping with your attorney will cost you money, so that's how you can utilize your family and friends. When you communicate with your lawyer, it makes more sense to write down what you want your attorney to know or questions you need to ask. If these facts are significant, tell the attorney directly, either in person or on the telephone. But many of the details of divorce are not earth shaking. They can be communicated by e-mail or relayed by the attorney's legal assistant or secretary.

Most matrimonial law experts charge a great deal for clients who call them at home or on weekends, just to vent their complaints. This is valuable family time for the attorney, and you should respect his or her privacy. Instead, talk to the secretary or legal assistant as often as possible. Let your attorney know you are doing that intentionally, so as not to waste his time and your money. If there is an emergency, though, it may be necessary to call your attorney at home. I make certain every client knows to call me at home if the need arises. But it should be a matter of great urgency that cannot wait until morning. For instance, you should not call when your spouse is 10 minutes late bringing home the children. You and your attorney should agree about what specifically constitutes an emergency.

How combative the opposing party gets can affect the cost of your case. If your spouse wants his or her day in court, or will not bend on the simplest property issues, you may be in for a lengthy and expensive battle. This type of opposing party will fight everything your attorney attempts to do in the case, resulting in significantly higher legal bills for both sides.

Pay The Initial Retainer

Most family attorneys require a retainer, which is a down payment that ensures the lawyer will be paid for time spent on the case. Retainers ranging from $750 to $15,000 are common in most areas of Alabama, although retainers up to $50,000 may be required in very complex cases. The highest retainers usually involve a complicated custody fight or complex property arrangement.

The retainer may only be a partial payment of the fees in the case, depending upon the time involved in completing the action. If the case settles without utilizing the entire retainer, or if the client decides to seek other legal representation, then the amount not applied to time spent on the case will be returned to the client.

Some lawyers handle cases on a flat fee arrangement instead of totaling hours. In those cases, the client will pay a fee ranging from several thousand to several hundred thousand dollars, no matter how many hours are expended on the case.

It is not unusual for an attorney facing trial to get a supplemental retainer to cover the expenses of being in court. If a client cannot find the money to pay the lawyer during the middle of a crisis, it is unlikely that he or she will pay the lawyer once the problem is solved. A contested trial may take several days or weeks of trial time to resolve, plus many hours of preparation. You need to prepare financially for these expenses. Fees and expenses can be substantial, and the attorney expects to be paid as the services are rendered, just like any other professional.

More than once, a divorcing person has called our office and said, "I don't have any money, so I can't afford to hire you, but would you answer some questions about my case?" This is similar to calling a doctor out of the blue, telling him that you have discovered a huge lump and wanting to know over the phone if it is cancer and how to remove it. Neither the lawyer nor the doctor can properly advise clients over the phone, based on limited facts and such a tenuous commitment by the person seeking the divorce.

If money to retain a lawyer is not readily available, you may have to consider other sources for payment of these funds. Advances on credit cards, bank notes or a short-term loan from a friend or relative are all possibilities. Most attorneys will not proceed in a case until the retainer is paid. So you may need to explore all the options to obtain the necessary funds.

With Gender Neutrality, Each Party Usually Pays Own Fees

If your spouse controls the family purse strings and you have to scrounge for living expenses, you would think the court would require the spouse with the money to pay your legal fees. If the fees are not awarded to your spouse, or if he or she fails to pay them, you are responsible for them. Most divorce experts require a client to pay the fees incurred before the case is resolved. Then if the other side is ordered to absorb the fees, the lawyer will reimburse the client once the balance is paid. In most cases, divorce experts will not take on a litigated divorce hoping the other side will pay the fees.

Some attorneys do file cases without having been paid, in the hope that the other spouse will pay their fees. Taking the case on that basis usually results in the lawyer not getting paid for a long time, or the client being left with a huge bill. If your lawyer has done a good job representing you, the other spouse will not be thrilled to pay money to the person who caused him or her so much difficulty.

Often, when considering how much money an effective divorce lawyer can cost them, people fail to recognize the enormous amount of money at stake in a divorce. This can include the cumulative value of child support and alimony, along with the related property settlement issues. The total can be staggering. For example, if a 35-year-old woman requests $1,500 per month in periodic alimony from her husband, the payments could easily total more than half a million dollars over her lifetime. Coupled with child support awards, property settlements, equity in the home, retirement plans, insurance considerations, debts, and college expenses, the value of an estate can range from several hundred thousand dollars to several million dollars in a divorce of middle class people. If you have that much money on the line, hiring a skilled matrimonial law specialist seems like a prudent investment.

Contingency Fees Aren't Legal in Family Law

"What do you mean I owe you money. The other lawyer's ad I saw on television said you get no money unless you collect."

An Anonymous Client

Don't confuse the billing practices of a divorce lawyer in Alabama with those of a personal injury attorney. The Alabama Rules of Professional Conduct prohibit contingency fees in divorce cases, except in very limited circumstances. Under a contingency arrangement you might make in an accident or injury case, an attorney is paid a percentage of the settlement award. The famous advertisement line that "you will pay no attorney's fees unless we recover" may apply to personal injury, but not to the legal fees in your divorce.

Since your divorce attorney will charge either a flat rate or hourly, it's important to find out what the attorney charges for his time and that of his associates and staff. Generally, the rule of thumb to follow is an age-old one; you get what you pay for. Most matrimonial law experts in Alabama charge from $100 to $250 and upwards per hour for their services, and $50 and up per hour for paralegals and other staff members.

Many lawyers across the country have begun billing litigation cases with what are called alternative billing methods. These methods can include a flat fee on a monthly basis renewed each month, where the first and last month's fees are paid up front. In addition, many lawyers have begun value billing their clients, whereby the lawyer and the client are able to agree on a bonus to be paid at the end of the case based on the results achieved. This is totally different from a contingency fee because it is only reached at the end of the case and through an agreement between the client and the party. For example, if a lawyer takes a case and saves the client $4,000,000 based on his experience and expertise, the parties may agree that the lawyer is entitled to a bonus at the end of the case. For the client who expects to receive money at the end of the case, if a lawyer gets him or her a significant increase in the settlement, the party and the lawyer may agree that a bonus is due. Many top business executives find this an attractive practice because they can further motivate the lawyer to concentrate on their case by rewarding them at the end based on the results achieved.

The typical hourly billing structure rewards the lawyer for consuming hours, while value billing pays for results. As they say in the Old West, gunfighters don't get paid by the bullet.

In other words, if an efficient lawyer can get your case resolved in an hour, he would be paid less than an inefficient lawyer who took 10 hours. If you think an alternative billing method may interest you, discuss it with your lawyer.

Ask For a Statement

Even in this day of the savvy legal consumer, some lawyers simply tell you the balance due at the end of the divorce. You should discourage this practice, because you may end up owing far more money than you expected. You should be kept abreast of the time incurred in your case on a monthly basis and keep track of the balance of any retainer. Legal time can quickly add up and surpass the value of the assets in question. If your spouse is overly difficult, your attorney will invest a lot of time in your case, and your fees will rise quickly. If your attorney does the work, you will be obligated to pay the fees regardless of the outcome. Many clients want the lawyer to do an enormous amount of work without realizing the tremendous costs associated with it. Therefore, make sure to request billing statements if your attorney does not provide them.

Preparing a case for trial may require the lawyer to work many hours preparing witnesses. Some clients are too quick to say they want their lawyer to do whatever it takes. This type of attitude can cost an incredible amount of money. And giving your attorney carte blanche authority to spend your money rarely produces a successful divorce. This type of client often compares the value of the settlement to the legal bills without considering the services performed by the lawyer.

Who Is Responsible For Expenses?

Most attorneys bill you separately for expenses incurred in the case, including filing fees and deposition costs. The attorney spends this money in the course of representation, and generally the amounts are due at the time the services are rendered. The average filing fee for a divorce action in Alabama is $154. Deposition costs are generally based on the length of the deposition. The lawyer pays a court reporter to record the testimony in the deposition. A typical divorce deposition will cost anywhere from $300 to $1,000 or more for the court reporter. This does not include the attorney's time associated with preparing for and taking the deposition.

Another expense is special process server fees. These are charges for serving the opposing party with pleadings, subpoenas and other related documents. If time is important, a special process server can serve the documents immediately, while the local sheriff's department sometimes takes several weeks. The fee for service of documents by a process server generally runs from $75 to $200 or more, depending upon the difficulty incurred in locating and serving the individual. Many law firms charge for copies and faxes as well as other costs associated with preparing the case. It is always wise to familiarize yourself with the anticipated costs to avoid confusion.

How Can You And Your Lawyer Help Each Other?

If you hire a lawyer after the initial meeting, you should know what steps your attorney plans to take next. For instance, you should know when he expects to file the divorce and when the other spouse will be served with papers. You should be kept abreast of the latest developments in the case, so you will be prepared if your spouse throws out some bit of information about the case. Your spouse may or may not retaliate in response to the divorce action, especially after being served with divorce papers. If the lawyer has a problem advising you of the action he or she will take, it may be an early indication of a communication problem.

The attorney will need to know the reasons for the divorce and the overall history of the marriage. This type of narrative can prove extremely helpful to the lawyer and his staff in preparing your case. It should be as detailed as possible.

Prepare this narrative at work or at a safe place where your spouse cannot find it. A detailed history of any sordid behavior would be extremely hard to explain if your spouse discovered it.

The lawyer will also need a detailed listing of assets and debts. And if custody is an issue, the lawyer will need extensive information on the children.

People going through a divorce often suffer from a Humpty Dumpty syndrome, thinking the lawyers or the judge can put their lives back together. The most anyone can hope for is to be left with the tools to do it themselves.

An Alabama Circuit Court Judge

CHAPTER SIX

When Mr. Right Becomes The Wrong Attorney For You

IF YOU AREN'T GOING TO GET ALONG with your attorney in a divorce, you will know very soon. For attorneys all across the country, inattention to detail is the greatest problem clients have with them.

He Doesn't Return Your Phone Calls

There is the story of a divorce attorney who went for months not returning repeated telephone calls from his client, who simply wanted to know about the progress of her case. Soon she gave up calling the attorney and began to ask for the legal assistant. The assistant continually referred her to the attorney, so the client was reduced to begging for news from the receptionist.

After more than six months had elapsed and the client had no notice that a divorce was filed, she began to send faxes and then letters to the attorney. Almost in a panic, she got creative. Telling the receptionist that it was she, the client, who had failed to call back the attorney, she wrangled the attorney's car phone number out of the receptionist. After several tries, she got him en route.

Without skipping a beat, the attorney said things were beginning to happen and that he was on his way to the courthouse on some vague matter dealing with her divorce.

"And I've been meaning to call you because we have a settlement offer from the other side," said the attorney.

"What does it say?" asked the client.

"I don't know," replied the attorney. "I haven't read it."

This is not the type of communication that results in a successful divorce.

Excitement Equals Increased Cost

Sometimes, an excited client can stir an attorney into too much action, resulting in wasted motion and money and, finally, an angry client.

A noted physician shopped around for the meanest lawyer in town to take on his soon-to-be ex-wife, whom he called a "crazy woman." When he found a divorce lawyer with his same glint of revenge in his eye, he retained the man and paid him a $25,000 retainer for a complex divorce with children involved.

Soon the lawyer had paper flying in the form of a divorce petition and numerous motions that contained all manner of accusations about his wife and the mother of his children. When the doctor called the attorney's office, he was put through immediately. He would engage the attorney in long, rambling conversations raging against his ex. The doctor even called the attorney on the weekend, including calls to his cellular number and the phone at his lake house.

With all of that action, the doctor had to replenish the retainer with another $25,000, then $50,000 more. Things were starting to happen, but it wasn't necessarily what the doctor expected. His in-laws, who were close to him before all of this, would not speak to him. And his children were so upset that he had to pay for counseling. The doctor's practice was suffering an unusual number of appointment cancellations, and the level of tension was so high that he had trouble sleeping.

Soon the doctor/client had enough. When he called to complain, the attorney reminded him that he said to "spare no expense," " be aggressive" and "make the other side miserable."

"But I also said to win," said his client. "I've spent $100,000 and I'm farther away from winning than I was when I started."

The doctor eventually learned the hard way about winning at all cost. He instructed the lawyer to handle the case in the proper, methodical fashion. Once tensions calmed, the parties were eventually able to settle the case. The moral of this story is that you need to follow your lawyer's advice and not set out to destroy the other side.

Evaluate Your Lawyer's Performance

Clients should constantly evaluate their lawyer's performance by these benchmarks: are you closer to a resolution of the divorce than you were when you hired him or her? Do you feel that you'll get anywhere close to what the attorney suggested you would get? Will you and the other side be able to deal with each other when the case is over? How much is this costing you?

At the same time, understand that your lawyer is not a magician and he cannot create miracles. If your spouse is difficult, the fees will increase. If nothing is happening in the case, you should not expect daily or weekly updates. Relaying such information will use up your retainer needlessly.

But if your lawyer is not making progress, you may have to consider retaining someone else. This is a drastic move, one you should make only after careful consideration. It can be expensive to constantly change attorneys, and oftentimes we find that people who change attorneys simply have unrealistic expectations. Changing attorneys without a very good reason can create the impression that the client is the difficult person, not the lawyer. But if you make the decision, making the change should not be difficult.

Simply call your lawyer and discuss your concerns in detail. If you want to get another attorney, call or write your attorney and ask him or her to send your file to you or another attorney. If you cannot reach him by phone, send him a fax or letter and call his office to confirm it. For the good of your case, it is best not to make the change when you are facing an immediate court appearance.

But whenever this happens, you should receive a refund of any retainer amount being held by the retiring attorney, or pay any existing balance due, subject to the terms of your fee agreement.

PART 2

The Heart of the Case

Whoever said that marriage is a 50-50 proposition laid the foundation for more divorce fees than any other short sentence in our language.

Austin Elliot

CHAPTER SEVEN

Win at Trial Before It Begins

HOW AGGRESSIVELY YOU PURSUE YOUR DIVORCE is a point of debate in almost every case. If you come on too strong, you might alienate someone you've lived with and loved, not to mention friends and other family members. If you approach the divorce meekly, you may be setting yourself up to be run over. Remember that there is life after divorce, and you will want to be in position to enjoy it.

Assert Yourself

Given these two choices, erring on the side of assertive action usually is the best way to reach a successful divorce. If some piece of property belongs to you, talk to your attorney about whether you need to get it out of the house. If your spouse's behavior endangers the children, and you can prove it, you also need to discuss with your attorney how to protect yourself and the children while the case is pending. Decisions like these should always be made after consultation with your attorney.

In a contested divorce, you must obtain as much information about the marriage as possible before your spouse is served notice of the divorce. A wealth of information is kept at home that can make or break your case at trial. Begin immediately accumulating as much information as possible regarding your financial affairs, as well as who is at fault for the divorce, without raising suspicion.

Obtain Family Information

Locating certain family information may help you establish crucial key evidence at trial. Obtain the past three to five years of the following information:

- Family photographs relevant to a custody battle
- Incriminating photographs - even if the other spouse is in the photo
- Love letters from your spouse to a third party
- Love letters from a third party to your spouse
- Any "secrets" of yours
- Any "secrets" of your spouse
- Personal tax returns
- Corporate tax returns
- Checking and savings account statements
- Financial records
- Medical records
- Substance abuse evidence or treatment records
- Brokerage or stock accounts
- Retirement account statements

- Mortgage information
- Credit card information
- Personal debt information
- Telephone records
- Long-distance telephone bills
- Cellular telephone bills
- Health insurance information
- Life insurance information
- Any other important financial information

This information may or may not be used at trial, but if possible it should be placed in a safe location that's not accessible to your spouse. If any of these records can damage your spouse's case, they may disappear if you don't have them in hand once the divorce is under way.

If a man pays for his girlfriend's hotel room with a credit card, the last thing he and his attorney will want is for that receipt to show up in court. Although adultery is not important in the divorce process in some states, it is still relevant in Alabama and can be a major factor for consideration of custody, alimony and property division. Keep whatever information you have in a safe place, because it may have to be turned over to the other side's attorney during the course of the litigation.

You should not construe this section as advising you to hide any information or assets, or that you will ultimately receive all of the assets just because you have them in your possession. On the contrary, you need to be as forthright as possible in the way you handle your case. If you hold key evidence at the beginning of a case, you will be more in control of the situation. The following discussion summarizes how some of this information can be used to your advantage or against you at trial, depending on the facts of your case.

Gather Financial Records

Many financial records contain information that only one spouse knows. For example, most bank accounts normally show paycheck deposits on the first and fifteenth day of each month. But a spouse may deposit substantially more money in a checking account on a monthly basis. Determining the origin of these funds will indicate the spouse's true monthly income.

In most cases, a spouse will claim his or her base salary is the only income. But if the person repeatedly deposits $25,000 a month in an account, while only claiming $10,000 in income per month, the history of these funds may be used to expose additional income from large commissions or bonuses. If the financial records reveal that the spouse has been taking advances from credit cards and other loans to meet monthly expenses, it may also indicate some unknown debts or perhaps a gambling problem.

Collect Long Distance and Cellular Phone Records

Most divorce lawyers will request both personal and business cellular phone and long distance records for the past three to five years. Collecting these long distance and cellular phone records may prove helpful in revealing an adulterous relationship. It is effective at trial to enlarge a long distance phone statement with page after page of calls to the same number. Once you identify the person being called, the lawyer simply poses the question, "What did you talk to Jane Doe about for seven hours from your car in one day?" Likewise, calls to illicit 900 sexual fantasy numbers can be very damaging at trial. Business phone records can also indicate if a spouse has been hiding certain calls behind company accounts, in addition to demonstrating he has been having an affair on company time. The information will prove very valuable and the guilty spouse may want to settle the case to keep his employer from finding out about a relationship that could affect his standing in his company.

Tell Your Attorney Your Secrets

While gathering incriminating evidence on a spouse, you also need to consider any evidence about yourself. There are two forms of client evidence likely to be harmful at trial. The first is the type of evidence the other spouse knows about, such as illegal drugs, incriminating photographs, sexual paraphernalia, videotapes and adulterous love letters. The second type is the evidence the other spouse doesn't know about, but can dig up, if given a chance.

Your spouse may not have concrete evidence of an adulterous relationship, but may attempt to obtain verification of the affair through a private investigator or standard discovery procedures, such as interrogatories and depositions. This affair may not be real, but will look that way.

I remember one client's spouse who was foolish enough to write checks for all of his girlfriend's bills from the family's joint account. He even wrote on the checks that they were for "Sharon's rent" or "Sharon's clothes." He had a lot of explaining to do at trial when he denied an adulterous relationship and said he did not know anyone named Sharon.

For some strange reason, people having affairs act like 16-year-olds who in love for the first time. The spouse having the affair abandons all logic and takes foolish risks in the name of love. Many people go to restaurants with a girlfriend or boyfriend, forgetting that the other spouse's friends may see them there. Also, taking that person to lunch during the workweek usually gives a secretary or other coworker knowledge of the person's whereabouts. They write love letters and leave them in a briefcase or purse. They also take pictures of each other together, and sometimes they begin buying lingerie or sexual devices.

Unearth Not-So Secrets

I remember one particular case in which a 50-year-old husband began going to a tanning salon, working out, and staying late at work every night. In time, his wife became suspicious of his activities. She determined that he had been going out of town and booking plane tickets in the girlfriend's name, calling the girlfriend daily on his cellular phone, charging local hotel bills on his credit card and writing checks to the girlfriend from the family joint account. The wife discovered most of this information before we got involved in the case. As difficult as it was to keep this secret, she did so until after we filed a complaint for divorce and made every effort to protect her and the marital assets.

If you are having an affair, do not assume that you are so good at keeping the secret that no one will ever know. Most talented private investigators can and will catch you if you are meeting your lover on a regular basis. If the police can catch professional criminals, it does not take a rocket scientist to catch a person going to the local motel with a girlfriend or boyfriend.

If you have been having an affair and a divorce is initiated, stop immediately. An amazing number of people seem compelled to continue seeing a paramour, even when they know their spouse is having them followed. Sometimes, it's as if the spouse wants to get caught, because he or she is so blatantly foolish. If you insist on continuing the relationship, just make sure it's worth the check you will have to write to settle the divorce.

If you suspect your spouse is having an affair, the collection of evidence concealed in your residence should be discussed with your attorney. Locating original documents that might prove the existence of an affair by your spouse can benefit you at trial. It also helps your lawyer, since he or she may not be able to get copies of key evidence admitted at trial, due to evidentiary limitations.

When searching for evidence, balance the fact that your spouse may become suspicious when certain things disappear. I have often advised clients not to worry about uncovering their spouse's secrets and angering them. It is doubtful the spouse will come out and say, "Honey, have you seen the naked pictures of my girlfriend? I was hiding them right here in my briefcase."

If violence is a possibility, be cautious if you start removing incriminating bits of evidence from your spouse's hiding places. The determination of how and when to get the evidence must be made on a case-by-case basis and should be made with the advice of your attorney.

Detail Sexual Misconduct

People have to recognize that during a divorce, evidence can be viewed from more than one perspective. For example, the most innocent and fun videotape or photograph of a sexual encounter with your spouse or paramour can become some of the most damaging evidence in a custody trial. Likewise, copies of phone bills with repeated calls to 900 sex-line numbers could enhance the opposing side's position in a custody battle. Be sure to discuss this evidence with your lawyer, so he or she can determine what should be done with it. Just because your spouse was involved in a particular sexual escapade does not always mean a slam dunk for you at trial. You still need to demonstrate an adverse affect on the children.

If both parties participated in some unusual sexual practice, the court can hold those parties equally responsible and may not put too much weight on the activity, unless the children were present. Since both parties were willing participants in the activity, it is not reasonable to hold one party at fault. Of course, the argument at trial usually centers on the justification that "I didn't want to do that and he made me do it." If the parties have participated in this activity many times over several years, that may be a difficult argument to sell. There is an exception. If one spouse has forced another to participate in undesirable activities, such as the use of some type of sexual device or some manner of forced sex, the court may not look kindly upon the forcing spouse.

Collect Photographs and Other Documentation of Abuse

In a divorce trial, a picture is unequivocally worth a thousand words. If a spouse is in an abusive situation, such abuse must be documented with photographs and medical reports that can be shown at trial. When the abusive spouse has left another spouse or their children bruised and beaten, these marks will be healed long before trial. Pictures of each bruise or abrasion should be taken immediately and medical treatment secured from an attending physician. You may have difficulty convincing a judge that the abuse took place if there are no photographs, medical records or police reports.

"If the abuse is reported to the police or Department of Human Resources, then someone from these agencies will take the pictures and document the abuse," says Detective John Lucas of the Mountain Brook Police Department. "However, pictures can also be taken by another family member or friend.

"I encourage spouses to report any abusive situation to the police and allow us to take care of the photos. A lot of times, in divorce cases, pictures can be taken so that they are not actually what they appear to be and it's better to have the support of law enforcement professionals."

If you need to file police reports, these should be made after consulting with your lawyer. Police officers and friends can be subpoenaed to testify to events they have witnessed.

There are many violent marriages that involve men who should be punished for their behavior. This type of behavior should not be tolerated. In most cases, the abused spouse exhibits such fear that a long history of abuse is apparent. However, some women say their husbands were abusive during the marriage, yet they don't want to hurt their feelings by having them arrested.

Wives like this rarely swear out a restraining order or have the husband forcibly removed from the home. In fact, she may continue sexual relations with the abusive spouse out of fear that he might harm her or her kids.

Of course, some people exaggerate the level of abuse in an attempt to better their case. This is a dangerous ploy that has no place in the divorce process. If you plead abuse to your attorney, you need to make certain the reported abuse has occurred and back it up with witnesses, photographs and police reports.

"After you've been doing it for a while, you can tell when it's an abusive situation," says Lucas. "I can look at the types of injuries to see if it's self inflicted. These situations are not always what they seem, but I think the flip side is more common, and more abuse goes unreported."

If you lie about an abusive situation at trial, and you are caught or the judge doesn't believe you, this type of behavior will adversely affect your case. So many people have lied about abuse in the past that the court is now automatically skeptical and requires significant proof to substantiate the abuse.

Hire a Private Investigator

In certain cases, especially those involving adultery or income questions, private investigation can be the most important aspect of a case. Do not hire a private investigator, though, without first calling your attorney. Your lawyer should have an investigator he or she trusts and recommends for your case. Unless the attorney hires the private investigator, the work may not be protected by the attorney/client privilege, and it may be more easily discoverable by the other side.

If the investigator catches your spouse with an extramarital friend, photographs and videotape may win your case. You can imagine the judge's reaction when you produce large photographs of your spouse kissing the person he or she supposedly never met.

"There's nothing more effective than a picture," says Jack Atkins, business manager for Divorce Investigation in

Birmingham. "Our main focus is to take pictures of our subject with the suspect. Our investigators are skilled at taking picture in any situation, in any light."

A fellow attorney once shared with me one of the most damaging private investigator stories. This attorney's investigator caught a mother in an adulterous relationship, having sex on videotape. The tape showed the mother having sex in a car, with the woman's young son beside them in the car seat. Obviously, the tape was very damaging to the mother's case at trial.

You should not pay to produce evidence you don't need. Depending on the facts of your case, the private investigator's report may be repetitive and simply back up evidence you already have. A private investigator may follow your spouse for several days to get the goods for you, and this will result in a substantial expense.

"Most cases can be made in three to seven days, but those are not consecutive days, because we have to establish a pattern," says Atkins. "When you show a pattern of adulterous behavior, it's very difficult to refute."

The cost of this investigation will be due immediately, regardless of whether the investigator has found any incriminating evidence. Even though you pay for it, the evidence may not be effective. Remember that a skillful trial lawyer can discredit many private investigators' reports due to flaws in their actions or experience as an investigator. As a result, many people squander money on a private investigator's report that may not add to the substance of the case.

Of course, an effective investigation could confirm something you might not have concluded otherwise, that your spouse is not having an affair and attempts to reconcile could bear fruit.

Using Tape Recorders

Before you hook up a tape recorder to your telephone, consult with your attorney. Strict laws protect people from being taped without their knowledge. Violations of these laws can result in criminal penalties and potentially damage your case. In limited circumstances, tape recording a conversation may be admissible if you are a party to that conversation. If you are not a party to that conversation, the tape almost always is inadmissible and illegal.

"We advise our clients to be very careful if they are taping a conversation, because it's a risky proposition," says Atkins. "We warn them that if they get caught recording a conversation, especially with their spouse, the snooping is all over. From then on, the other party will be guarded when talking to you."

Many judges do not like to deal with tape recordings of the other spouse during a divorce trial. They may view these recordings as spying. But because your spouse denies certain behaviors, a tape recording may be your only way to establish the truth.

If your spouse has been mentally or physically abusive toward you or your children, a tape recording can be damaging at trial. Whether or not you use a tape recording should be determined on a case-by-case basis. Certain cases warrant taping when there is no other way to establish certain points at trial. If you already have the other party on tape admitting a critical fact, it is very difficult for them to deny it at trial.

Evidence About You

Anyone going through a divorce should assume the other side is collecting the same kind of evidence you are gathering. Many cases have been lost because a spouse mistakenly felt his or her spouse did not have a clue about what he had done. In reality, that spouse had several clues, and may have gotten multiple pieces of evidence because of foolish mistakes. To reemphasize the point made earlier, be completely honest with your attorney about what you have done.

I can recall every client who has directly lied to me about a particular issue. If a client denies an adulterous relationship and is then shown in a video in bed with a paramour, we have a problem. Usually, our only recourse is to withdraw from representing the lying client. To avoid this problem, tell your lawyer the truth as early and often as possible.

Your quest for a successful divorce continues throughout the case, and you should not give the other side ammunition to shoot back at you at trial or in settlement discussions. Behave, and don't be in a hurry to begin dating. In fact, don't do anything to jeopardize your case. Don't fight, don't drink, don't date, don't do anything that your mother or minister would not condone. Many divorcing people feel their spouses get to have affairs and they cannot even go out to dinner while the divorce is pending. I do not care if it is an innocent dinner date with your best friend of the opposite sex during the pending divorce, it should not happen. You do not want the other side's lawyer bringing up the date at trial, making it seem like something torrid when it isn't. You may find it impossible to convince a judge you are upset about the breakup of your marriage when you are already dating.

If custody is at issue, you do not want the other side asserting that while he or she was at home with the children, you were out drinking in a bar with someone. Even the most innocent situation with a good friend can be construed in a negative light. Trust me.

A talented divorce lawyer with some ammunition can make Mary Poppins look like a tramp.

To detract from their fault, the other side may try to cloud the main issues before the court. Your spouse may know you are not having an affair. But if he is having one, you can bet he will try to show you are also guilty of dating, to minimize the harm caused by his adulterous relationship. Plenty of clients have their cases won, only to lose them by their actions during the divorce proceedings.

Establish Household Needs

Appendix B includes a chart that should help you determine your living expenses. At trial, you must have receipts and other documentation to confirm the validity of expenses listed on this form. It is important to balance your needs with your wants and desires. For example, many couples cannot afford to run a single household on two incomes, much less split the expenses of two separate households. Even if you think you must live in a mansion, you may have to adjust your standard of living to deal with the realities of divorce.

"When we are figuring our household budget, we tend to forget additional items that come up on an infrequent basis," says William B. Stapp, Certified Public Accountant for the accounting firm of Stapp and Stapp, PC in Selma. "When looking at a household budget, I recommend that people look at an entire year and then possibly another year back."

From this information, you should be able to estimate your present and future expenses. A lawyer needs these before he or she can determine the financial support necessary for your future welfare or your ability to pay support to your spouse. Often, this is a difficult challenge, because many clients are not familiar with their family's finances.

"It's always important to make sure you grasp how you really live," says Stapp. "Sometimes, there is a level of denial in that people think they are better off or that they make more money than they do. But, they don't have perspective on what they need day-to-day, like they should."

Lawyer: *What is your name?*
Witness: *Ernestine McDowell.*
Lawyer: *And what is your*
marital status?
Witness: *Fair.*

CHAPTER EIGHT

Mediation

ONE OF THE BEST WAYS to a successful divorce may be through mediation. Over the past decade, there has been a trend toward the use of alternative dispute resolution instead of litigation all across the country. Today, there are mediators who specialize in family mediation, while others handle business disputes as well as divorce.

It's Usually Voluntary

In many ways, mediation is a form of the same settlement process attorneys have engaged in since the judicial system began. You still have the two attorneys present as advocates for their clients. However, the parties and their attorneys are placed in separate rooms, and a neutral trained mediator moves from room to room aiding the parties in resolving their differences.

In some jurisdictions, families must participate in mediation before the court will hear the divorce case. In Alabama, mediation is usually voluntary. If either side requests it, though, and is willing to pay for it, mediation will be ordered in certain types of cases.

Mediation usually is not binding on the parties unless a settlement agreement is signed. But it has great advantages in cases where the parties can agree upon a middle ground. Using mediation to settle a divorce case can be less expensive, because you avoid most of the discovery process, preparation for trial and the actual time in court. Should the process founder, the parties lose a minimal amount of time and money compared to the potential costs of litigation. Successful mediation, however, oftentimes leaves parties more pleased with the outcome because they reach it on their own, rather than having it forced on them by a judge.

The Mediator's Job

A divorce case goes to mediation when the judge instructs the parties to attend or the people involved decide to use this method. If a judge requests mediation, he or she submits a list of qualified mediators to the parties and gives them the option to pick one.

Usually, the parties are sequestered in separate rooms with their attorneys and the mediator shuttles from one room to another. The mediator acts as the connecting point, relaying areas of agreement between the parties and feeling the parties out on some areas where disagreement could turn into a settlement.

"My role as a mediator is to thoroughly review the case so I can determine all the issues involved in the divorce, whether it's child custody, finances or home ownership," says Doug Key, managing partner and mediator with Key, Greer, Frewley, Key and Harrison in Pelham. He then begins to work with the parties to help them resolve matters in dispute.

"Within every mediation session, there's an opportunity for accord on some topic," Key says. "It's not the mediator's job to offer financial or legal advice of any kind. All parties work through their attorneys to agree on what is best for them."

In complex cases, mediation may take more than one day to finalize a settlement. If, at the end of the day, an agreement is reached, the lawyers formalize it into a settlement agreement that the parties execute and file with the court.

All across the nation, mediation settles as many as one-half of all cases, thereby reducing the logjam at the courthouse. And even when it doesn't settle everything, often it reduces the number of issues to decide. At its worst, it still leaves people with the feeling that they tried the most rational means before submitting to the more abrasive court process.

There are three sides to every divorce case — his side, her side and the truth.

An Alabama Circuit Court Judge

CHAPTER NINE

Building A Strong Case Through Discovery

THE PROCESS OF FORMAL DISCOVERY allows both parties in a divorce to obtain additional information from the other side. These discovery procedures involve responding to specific requests from the opposing party. The procedures include written interrogatories, requests for production of documents, request for admissions, depositions and other forms of examination. In a perfect world, the parties would exchange relevant documents without a formal request. But it is fairly common that one side forces the other to provide even basic information such as checking account statements and tax returns.

An uncontested divorce or an extremely short marriage with few assets may not require discovery, but it is essential in most divorces. If you fail to discover other assets your spouse may have had or fault attributed to him or her, a judge usually won't give you a break if it is understood that you had an opportunity to discover this information and failed to pursue it.

The information you garner from discovery may be helpful for your case, or you may spend money and get nothing. You want to uncover what's pertinent without going on a wild goose chase.

The following discussion briefly summarizes the basic forms of discovery your lawyer may utilize during your case.

Interrogatories

Interrogatories are written questions asked of the other party to discover certain facts regarding the case. Answers to interrogatories must be prepared and filed within a prescribed period of time and given under oath. The interrogatories usually relate to employment and salary information, bank account information, charge accounts, assets and debts. There may be questions concerning adulterous relationships, abuse of a spouse or children, use of illegal drugs or other behavioral problems. If any fault questions apply to you, discuss them with your attorney to determine the best way to respond. The answers must be updated prior to trial, if there are any changes.

The court does not look favorably upon a party who lies in the interrogatory responses. Proof of these lies during the trial may greatly affect the outcome. At the same time, don't expect a judge to be shocked that the other side was less than truthful. Many spouses lie on a regular basis during their divorce, and it may be difficult to get the court to punish the responsible party.

Request for Production of Documents

A request for production of documents is often served when the opposing party is asked to answer the interrogatories. The requests contain specific demands for documents to prepare the case. One party usually requests three to five years worth of bank statements, tax returns, charge statements, business records, insurance information, financial data and numerous other kinds of information, including any evidence that the party plans to use at trial.

Your attorney will examine this information to determine which documents are relevant. If one spouse fails to provide information to the other, this may prevent either side from using it at trial. There is no quicker way to impact the other side at trial than to object to the admission of a key piece of evidence because you never saw it. For instance, you might properly request that your spouse provide profit and loss statements on a business that is part of the marital property. If your spouse runs the business, keeps the records and simply fails to answer, the court will often prevent either of you from producing the records and using them as evidence at trial.

Request for Admissions

Requests for admissions contain questions the opposing party must admit or deny. These requests are used to shortcut the discovery process to immediately determine the opposing party's fault in the case. For example, your attorney may ask the opposing party to admit or deny an extramarital affair during the marriage. A guilty party is positioned in a delicate situation when asked this question. To admit the adultery may concede a fact that you might have trouble proving at trial. If he or she denies the adultery and you successfully prove it at trial, that person has not only committed adultery, but perjury as well. In addition, there are strict time limits for answering a request for admission. A failure to answer the requests for admission in a timely fashion may cause the requests to be deemed admitted by the trial court. Therefore, the opposing party cannot simply avoid answering questions without additional consequences.

The use of these requests on a widespread basis is fairly new here in Alabama. We were one of the first divorce firms to recognize their effectiveness, but today you are likely to ask for and answer requests for admissions in your divorce case.

Depositions

In many divorce cases, a deposition is necessary to find out the basis of the opposing party's case or the substance of a witness' testimony. A deposition is taken out of court, under oath, in the presence of a court reporter, typically at one of the lawyer's offices. The lawyer taking the deposition will usually ask the other side questions about the facts of the case and the history of the marriage.

There are numerous strategies for handling a deposition. At the very least, your attorney should advise you about the impact of a particular deposition on your situation. Your spouse may attempt to use a deposition to reveal each and every aspect of your case. A deposition of this importance could potentially make or break your case at trial, depending on the facts of your argument. It is critical that your attorney fully prepare you for your deposition. When a deposition becomes this important, the pressure and intensity of the moment can lead you to forget key information from your case. Your deposition should include all the reasons you want the divorce. You should not only prepare for the initial deposition, but review before trial what you said in that deposition.

Additionally, a deposition can be used to discredit a witness if he changes his testimony at trial. Good lawyers employ the deposition process to size up the opposing party and their case to determine how they will appear on the witness stand. Lawyers often try to trick the other side at trial by saying something like, "that's not what you said at your deposition." Many times, the lawyer himself does not remember what the opposing party said in the deposition, but simply wants to test the witness' memory. If the lawyer believes the witness was lying, he may attempt to confuse the witness in hopes that he could not remember which story he gave in the deposition.

Certain cases warrant a deposition and others do not. Every deposition requires a court reporter, which results in additional expenses, such as the lawyer's preparation time. Before you begin the deposition process and spend the money, be certain that settlement is not possible. Some lengthy depositions can cost from $500 to several thousand dollars when you calculate the cost for a court reporter and your attorney's time for preparation and taking the deposition.

Consider the issue at hand. A bank account with a minimal amount of money in it may not be worth the cost of a deposition, regardless of the information gathered. If the assets are not known or if custody is at issue, a deposition could be necessary, unless the information can be obtained through other means.

Snow White doesn't marry Hitler,
and no one party is 100% at fault.

Anonymous divorce attorney

CHAPTER TEN

Deciding Who's at Fault

ALABAMA DOES NOT HAVE an actual no-fault divorce statute. This means the fault of the parties in the breakup of the marriage can be used by the judge as a factor in determining the division of marital property and deciding the custody of children. When a divorce is uncontested, however, one party can allege incompatibility, and this basically serves as a form of no-fault divorce.

Judges Must Decide

Most divorce court judges in Alabama would rather not have to consider fault. Imagine yourself in their position, listening day after day to the squabbling and fighting of supposed adults. They hear highly personal matters in open court. Most judges would prefer that cases settle outside of court. But under Alabama law, they are allowed to use fault as a basis for property division and the awarding of alimony or custody.

If there is no fault present and the parties have merely grown apart, the court usually will attempt to equitably divide the assets and debts of the parties. Alabama is one of the 40 states that provides for the equitable division of assets as a provision of state law (The remaining 10 states have community property statutes).

Equitable division does not always mean equal division. The judge determines, based on the facts, what kind of division is fair and equitable. If one spouse has been primarily responsible for the breakup of the marriage, the court has the discretion to compensate the other spouse with a greater division of the property or by awarding alimony. At the same time, one spouse will not necessarily receive the lion's share of the marital assets simply because there is fault. This depends on numerous factors, including the type of fault, the length of the marriage, and the assets and debts in question.

Types of Fault

The following list summarizes the various forms of fault often considered by the trial court in a divorce:

- Adultery
- Drug use
- Alcoholism
- Physical abuse of a spouse
- Mental abuse of a spouse
- Physical abuse of a child
- Mental abuse of a child
- Sexual abuse of a child
- Gambling

- Excessive spending
- Mental illness and psychological problems
- Criminal convictions
- Unusual sexual practices

Fault Must Be Proven

The fault of another party must be proven to a judge in court. You may believe your spouse has been having an affair. But when asked what evidence you have about the liaison, you cannot simply respond, "Oh, I know he's been sleeping with her, he just acts like he has." You need more than a gut feeling, speculation and rumor, which are not admissible in court, to establish the facts at trial. On the other hand, you are not likely to catch your spouse actually in bed with another person. But you still need to develop some kind of concrete proof to establish your spouse's guilt.

The courts often utilize what is called the reasonable person's standard, weighing the cumulative effect of all the evidence. The judge often asks whether the evidence indicates the behavior of a married person properly executing familial duties. Most married people are not seen in bars late at night with another person of the opposite sex. Few go to that person's apartment several times each week or make hundreds of cellular phone calls to the person late at night. In this type of situation, most divorce lawyers place the burden on the accused party to explain all of these circumstances. Remember, your judge will probably be married and possess a keen sense of what actions are reasonable and unreasonable in a marriage.

If you are guilty, you need to consider how your actions will look. You and your lawyer can decide how to address these issues.

For a couple with young children, divorce seldom comes as a solution to stress, only as a way to end one form of pain and accept another.

Fred (Mister) Rogers

CHAPTER ELEVEN

Fighting for Custody of Children

WE HAVE A POLICY AT MY OFFICE that exonerates children for any fault in the divorce. Regardless of what brought the parents into this arena, the children are innocent bystanders. We will not participate in a case if our client insists on badgering the children.

When minor children are involved, the custody of those children is of paramount importance in the divorce. Every parent always wants to know the answer to the question, "Will I get my children in the divorce?" Sometimes the issue is moot, because one of the parties has already conceded custody of the minor children to the other spouse.

The Fight of Your Life

When custody is contested, prepare for total war. Nothing is more contentious than a full-blown custody battle. Until recently, women routinely received custody of the children, especially infant children. But there has been a paradigm shift in the courtrooms in many Alabama jurisdictions, and men are walking into custody trials on a more level playing field. Because of these changing times, men are winning custody of the kids in increasing numbers.

I recently represented a man in a small rural county. He had been informed by his previous attorney that no man in that county had ever won custody of his children. He was convinced that his wife had a serious drug problem and posed a danger to the child. Through his testimony, coupled with three experts who testified to the mother's drug addiction, he was awarded custody of his five-year-old daughter.

In another case, I represented a man who drove a bulldozer for a living. He was awarded custody of a newborn and two older children based on his wife's misconduct. Many mothers believe that because they are moms, they cannot lose. Usually, I tell clients that because they are female, they begin with a 10-point lead in the custody game, but unfavorable conduct can quickly diminish that lead. Our judges want to see children placed in the best possible environment. In my experience, I have seen good moms and good dads, bad moms and bad dads. Each custody case is unique due to the facts, circumstances and fault surrounding the breakup of the marriage, as well as each parent's individual relationship and role with the children during and after the marriage. Make certain your lawyer is aware of all potential issues that could be raised concerning your conduct, so that custody is not at risk in your case.

Retaliating By Seeking Custody

Some fathers fight for custody simply to retaliate against the mother or to force her to give in on financial issues rather than risk a trial over custody. Some women threaten fathers with limited visitation to gain an economic advantage. Most spouses can determine if the other spouse is serious about receiving custody. If so, custody should take priority throughout the divorce process.

The noncustodial parent's role with the children after the divorce usually mirrors what that parent's role was beforehand. If the marriage was a traditional one, where the father spent less time with the children than his wife prior to the divorce, it is doubtful that he will instantly become heavily involved in his children's lives. But if this was a two-wage-earner family, as most are these days, both mother and father probably had their absentee periods. After divorce, this relationship will probably continue. Despite what caused the breakup, the children deserve to have the best possible relationship with both parents following the divorce. In addition, the noncustodial parent is more likely to pay child support and assist with other expenses related to the child if he or she sees the children regularly.

"The impact of the divorce on the children continues to affect me," says an Alabama Circuit Court Judge. "The children deserve to continue to have two parents."

Sole v. Joint Custody

The court awards two types of custody: either sole custody to one parent or joint custody to both. Most divorcing couples misunderstand these custody terms and what each spouse's rights are under the custody arrangement. Initially, you might think joint custody is a great idea. You may change your mind once the arrangement is explained to you. It is sad and ironic how many people call me after they have signed their divorce papers and want to change the custody terms because their lawyer did not explain the terms to them. The following summarizes the differences between joint and sole custody and the rights of the parents under each.

Under a sole custody arrangement, one parent has the legal right to the care, custody and control of the minor children. The other parent is awarded specific visitation rights with the children. This means the children live with the parent who is awarded sole custody. That parent has the right and responsibility for making all major decisions relating to the children, including medical, educational, academic and social matters.

Standard Visitation

Some parents forget that their children are not pieces of furniture that can be moved in and out of a house without concern. The court strives to stabilize the children, sometimes at the expense of the parents' comfort, setting up a standard visitation schedule. Many custodial parents have problems allowing the other parent to have even minimum visitation with the children.

The court wants to foster the relationship of the children with the noncustodial parent. Unless you can prove that seeing this parent will harm the children, usually the judge will not restrict or limit the noncustodial parent's visitation beyond the standard visitation schedule. Generally, the court provides three separate visitation schedules, depending on the age of the children. The courts have determined that visitation should vary for children under 12 months of age, from one year to three years and over three years of age. The complete visitation schedules are listed in Appendix E. These schedules may differ slightly for each jurisdiction. Consult your attorney for the specific language applicable to you.

Out-of-State Visitation

If the noncustodial parent lives out of state, the parties may select, or the noncustodial parent may be awarded, out-of-state visitation, a different schedule enacted due to the difficulty following the above standard visitation schedules. The out-of-state schedule is primarily tailored to long distance situations where airline travel is required.

In 2003, the Alabama Parent-Child Relationship Protection Act went into effect. This new law requires a relocating parent with custody to notify the nonrelocating parent 45 days before moving the child more than 60 miles or to another state. The notice to the nonrelocating parent must include the following:

- Address and phone number of the new residence and of the new school the child will attend
- The date of the move
- The specific reason for the move
- A proposed plan for altering custody and visitation
- A warning that the nonrelocating parent must object to the move within 30 days or the move will be allowed.

The nonrelocating parent must file the objection with the court and request a hearing. The objection can come in the form of a request to modify custody or visitation schedules. Pending the hearing, the judge may delay the move. Both sides may present evidence at the hearing that the move either will or won't benefit the child. The law sets up what is called a rebuttable presumption that the move is not in the best interest of the child, but evidence to the contrary can overcome that presumption. The judge has the power to change custody or visitation, and that fact strikes fear in the hearts of custodial parents all across Alabama.

If the nonrelocating party does not take action seeking a temporary or permanent order to prevent the move within the 30-day time frame, the change of residence is automatically authorized.

The Relocation Act will be included in every upcoming custody agreement or modification, but it can also be interpreted to affect existing custody orders. If you are considering a move, it is important that you take note of this new law. Some moves that require notification are surprising to parents. The mother (custodial parent) of two children lives in Birmingham, while the father (noncustodial parent) lives in Mobile. The mother decides to relocate to Pensacola, Florida. Even though the father's commute to visit his children is greatly reduced by the move, the mother still has to give notice because the move is out of state.

At this writing, this Act is in effect but is certain to be contested. Supporters of this legislation believe the child's right to access to both parents is paramount. Critics say the law restricts the right of the relocating parent to free movement and is unconstitutional for that reason. Similar legislation in other states has been struck down.

What is Joint Custody?

Joint custody once was considered a panacea for all the ills brought on by divorce. In theory, joint custody allows both parents to retain some control over their children's lives. In addition, it alleviates the stigma many parents feel when they give up custody of their children or have it taken away by the courts. Alabama recently passed a statute authorizing the courts to award joint custody to both parents if it is in the best interest of the children. But don't confuse the legal designation of joint custody with actual, physical joint custody.

In numerous ways, joint custody in this state is similar to sole custody. In many cases, it creates problems surrounding the care and control of the children. As a result, most judges and divorce attorneys do not like joint custody and only recommend it in limited circumstances where the parents are likely to agree on post-divorce issues.

Under a joint custody arrangement in this state, one parent usually is designated the primary custodian and the other parent is the secondary custodian. The children live with the primary custodian except for the time they visit the other parent under a specified schedule. Traditionally, most joint custody arrangements specify that parents make joint decisions concerning the children.

But many agreements also say that when parents cannot agree on academic, medical, religious and other issues, one party must exercise the power to resolve disputed issues. The parent with the final authority on a particular issue may override the other parent's request every time. This veto power can create tremendous conflict in post-divorce situations. For example, the primary custodial parent often retains final authority for academic decisions, since the child lives with that parent. The secondary custodial parent has the right to a voice in academic decisions, but the primary custodian has the final say on disputed issues. If a dispute arises concerning whether the children shall attend public or private schools, the parent with the authority over the academic decisions will have the right to make the final decision every time.

One of the primary reasons many family law experts do not favor joint custody is that it tends to push parents together in a false sense of cooperation. This degree of collaboration may be possible between two married parents, but generally couples getting a divorce have little or no ability to agree on even the simplest issues. Furthermore, the label of joint custody often creates a misconception between parents who do not understand their actual legal rights under the custody arrangement. Many parents believe joint custody means that both parents retain an equal vote on all decisions concerning the children. This is far from the truth and can lead to a shocking realization after the divorce. Joint custody only works under the following conditions; when parents have a good relationship with their children, are willing to make sacrifices to enrich their children's lives and are able to communicate with each other.

Sample Joint Custody Language and Visitation Provisions

The following language contains the typical terms contained in a joint custody agreement. Pay particular attention to this language, and if you apply this to any real life scenario, you will see the host of potential problems that could arise.

It is agreed by the parties that it is in the best interest of the children, Kate Doe and Jack Doe, for their care, custody and control, to be shared by both parties. The husband and wife understand that shared custody means both parties shall retain full parental rights and responsibilities with respect to their children, regardless of which party has physical custody at any particular time. The husband and wife agree that shared custody means shared parental responsibility and requires both parents to confer so that major decisions affecting the health and welfare of the children will be jointly determined. (Either party can be designated as the primary custodian, but this example assumes the wife is the primary custodian.)

(A) Schedule. The wife shall be the primary custodian and shall maintain the primary residence for the children, and the husband shall be the secondary custodian and shall maintain the secondary residence for the children. The secondary custodian's custodial periods shall be as follows:

(1) The first and third weekends of each month from 6 p.m. on Friday until 6 p.m. the following Sunday. The first weekend shall begin on the first Friday of each month at 6 p.m.;

(2) Each Christmas Day from 3 p.m. until 3 p.m. on the following New Year's Day;

(3) Thirty-one days during the summer (to be taken between June 10 and August 15) to be selected by the non-custodial parent, but upon written notice to the custodial parent at least 30 days in advance of such visitation;

(4) During the odd years, spring break vacation from 9 a.m. Saturday until the following Friday at 6 p.m.;

(5) During the even years, Thanksgiving vacation from Wednesday at 6 p.m. until Sunday at 6 p.m.;

(6) Every other birthday of the child from 6 p.m. on said date until 8 a.m. the following morning;

(7) Every Father/Mother's Day from 9 a.m. until 6 p.m. of the same day;

(8) On the birthday of the mother/father from 3 p.m. on said date until 8 p.m. of the same day;

(9) Any other reasonable times and places upon which the parties can agree; and

(10) Each party shall keep the other informed on a current basis as to the primary residence, address and telephone number where the children reside or visit.

(B) Activities of the minor children. Both the husband and wife desire to be involved in the various activities of their minor children. These include academic, religious, civic (such as Scouts or other civic-related organizations or community projects), cultural (such as music, theater, and the like), athletic, purchase of clothing, and medical and dental activities of the children. The husband and wife agree to cooperate with the other in adjusting their schedules to assure that the children are delivered to and returned from any such activity. It is further agreed and understood that both parties will notify one another of all conferences, programs, or events relating to such activities in such a way that both parties will have an opportunity to participate in such activities of the children.

Should the husband and wife be unable to agree on any aspect of the academic, religious, civic, cultural, athletic, or medical and dental activities of the children, the following party is hereby designated as having the primary authority and responsibility regarding involvement in said activity:

- Academic Wife (Can select Husband or Wife)
- Religious Wife (Can select Husband or Wife)
- Civic Husband (Can select Husband or Wife)
- Cultural Husband (Can select Husband or Wife)
- Athletic Husband (Can select Husband or Wife)
- Medical/Dental Wife (Can select Husband or Wife)

The exercise of this primary authority is in no way intended to negate the responsibility of the parties to notify and communicate with each other.

How to Determine the Primary Custodian

In a custody dispute, it is important to illustrate to the court that one parent has been the primary custodian of the children throughout the marriage. This parent usually is the one who receives primary custody of the children after the divorce, unless there are significant conflicting circumstances. To determine who is the primary custodian, you need to determine who performs most of the following activities for the children:

- Who helps the children get dressed for school?
- Who fixes breakfast for the children?
- Who packs the children's lunch for school?
- Who helps the children with their homework?
- Who participates in school activities with the children?
- Who takes care of the children after school?
- Who bathes the children?
- Who takes the children to school?
- Who takes the children to the doctor?
- Who takes the children shopping?
- Who takes the children to religious activities?
- Who arranges the children's extracurricular activities?
- Who helps children in various stages of development?

What a Parent Should Know Before Custody Battle

Before entering into a custody battle, make certain you know answers to basic questions concerning the care of your child. Any parent who has participated in the majority of the activities necessary to meeting the basic needs of a child should be able to answer the following questions:

- Who is the child's doctor?
- Where is his/her office?
- What allergies does the child have?
- Who is the child's dentist?
- Who is the child's principal?
- Who is the child's teacher?
- What is the child's favorite subject in school?
- Who is the child's day care provider?
- How often does the child go to day care?
- Name the child's three best friends.
- What is the child's favorite book?
- What is the child's favorite color?
- What special needs does the child have?
- What size shoe does the child wear?
- What size clothes does the child wear?

Sometimes a parent who means well, but hasn't taken an active role in the care of children, needs time to establish a role with the child and learn critical information before asking for custody. One client who came into our office was convinced his wife was mentally unstable and could no longer care for their son. Although he worked long hours and traveled for his company, he was determined to make a change in his life. For months, he strengthened his position with the child and kept a journal of his wife's erratic behavior.

After a particularly disturbing weekend at home, the father alerted us to file the divorce, and he moved the child elsewhere for protection. Because he was well prepared and could demonstrate how his wife's mental state was affecting his son, the man won sole custody of the child and the wife received limited visitation.

Potential Custody/Visitation Problems

"I have always told my son the truth. I think it is important to let him know that his mother is a fat alcoholic." This was the straight-faced declaration of the father of a five-year-old. Doesn't this sound as though the father's pain will cause visitation problems in the future? I am a firm believer that the children do not need to know every issue in a divorce.

If young children are involved in the divorce, I can practically guarantee there will be visitation problems in the future. No settlement agreement can address every potential circumstance that arises in the raising of children. Disputes may involve the simplest of issues. You may be a parent who cannot pick up the child at a scheduled time, due to unforeseen circumstances. Or your child may have an important event during a visitation period and the other parent refuses to take the child to the event. There are divorces without these problems, but they seem to be the exception.

Clients often call our office in a panic because an ex-spouse is 10 minutes late returning the child from visitation. One domestic judge asked the attorneys involved in a visitation dispute like this if their clients had lost their minds. In some instances, clients do feel they are losing their minds because of all the emotions involved. Why would anyone get the court involved because the ex brought the child home 10 minutes late? Plenty of married couples run late. Yet, when a court order spells out a visitation schedule, parents believe they can make absolutely no exceptions to the rule. Ten minutes may seem like a major infraction to that parent. But in the scheme of things, life goes on.

In some instances, noncustodial parents have not been allowed to take children to events such as baseball or football games, because the games were not during a visitation period. It is no wonder the two parents ended up divorced, when they are not able to squelch their harsh feelings for each other long enough to allow a child to attend a baseball game. Even worse, one parent will tell the child, "Yes, I would like to let you go to the game, but I can't trust your father to bring you home on time." Now, the child has not only been denied an opportunity to be with the other parent, but he has been placed in the middle of a petty visitation dispute.

Children Deserve Both Parents

"Children spell love 'T-I-M-E'." This is a wonderful quote from John Croyle, founder of the Big Oak Ranch Children's Home.

Children in a divorce deserve an equivalent amount of guidance from both parents. They don't need two parents who use them as pawns against each other. I am amazed at the number of parents who say they are honest with their child, so they explain to the child, "your mother was having an affair and she left us for someone else." A child or five or six years old is not mature enough to understand divorce. Most of the time, a parent is simply trying to turn the child against the other parent by filling the child's head with negative images.

Dr. Karen Turnbow, with Alabama Psychotherapy and

Wellness Center in Birmingham, has counseled separating families through divorces for the past 21 years. She recommends that parents only tell the children what they absolutely need to know about the divorce and save the details for themselves.

"I think parents need to be fairly general when they are talking about the divorce with their children," says Dr. Turnbow. "Children don't need to know that dad had an affair or mom charged up the credit cards. Divorcing couples should tell their children that sometimes parents have problems and can no longer live together in a peaceful, happy way."

I will never forget a case I had where a mother talked so badly about the father all week long that when it came time for his weekend visitation, the children didn't want to go. When confronted, the mother said she could not understand why the children would not go. Eventually, it was shown that the mother had talked so poorly about the father that the children truly believed he was a terrible monster. Besides speaking negatively about their father, the mother gave the children a tape recorder to record their father at the front door when he came to pick them up. She wanted to prove that he always lied to them. But this man was no monster. On the contrary, he was a wonderful individual and a good father with only his children's best interest in mind.

When he sued for custody, the children testified that they loved their father very much, but they did not want to hurt their mother's feelings by going with him. So they just didn't go on the visitation. The mother was found in contempt of court for willfully interfering with a divorce decree and was sentenced to jail. That mother should have lost custody for the example she set. She not only taught the children to lie, but she also created a barrier that nearly destroyed the father's relationship with the children. If not for the father's persistence, he would have had to give up on his children altogether. This example illustrates how children get enlisted to carry on the other parent's battle by refusing to visit their noncustodial parent.

"When this happens and a child refuses to visit another parent, that's when you need to seek the help of a professional," says Dr. Turnbow.

When this type of situation arises, I do everything I can to ensure that people do not use their children as pawns during and after a divorce. There are always differences of opinion over who is the better parent, but those disputes should remain between the parents. As a rule, I only put a child on the witness stand when the client and I have made a decision that, due to the overwhelming need for the testimony, we have no other choice.

Lawyers who put a child on the stand merely to ask a five-year-old which parent he or she wants to live with are making a strategic error most judges detest and often won't forgive. Many times, I question whether the parties and their lawyers know the destructive power they hold and the damage they can do to a child by involving them in the divorce decision making.

"No matter how old children are, they cannot decide where they will live," says Dr. Turnbow. "A lot of children do not want to make that decision. Saying that you want to live with one parent may make them feel like they are being disloyal to the other parent."

Remember that for most of your children's lives, they will remember how you handle the divorce. If you neglect them, they will never forget it. If you use them as pawns, they will never overlook it, nor are they likely to ever forgive you. One day they will grow up, and the games their parents played with their lives will become more apparent.

If you are looking out for your children's best interest, you will always separate your children from the divorce, even if it means tremendous personal sacrifice on your part. To do otherwise would harm not only your children, but your own self worth.

Divorce is the one human tragedy that reduces everything to cash.

Rita Mae Brown

CHAPTER TWELVE

Child Support

IN ALABAMA, child support is calculated by the state's child support guidelines, which must be followed in all cases involving children under the age of 19. Before passage of the guidelines, child support was calculated in a variety of ways, and some judges and parties even waived support in many cases. But the law is clear now that child support must be paid and cannot be waived, even with a parent's consent. The money belongs to the child, not the custodial parent, so parents cannot decide to excuse its payment. Only in limited circumstances will the court even consider a reduction in child support when the noncustodial parent spends extra time with the child, has travel expenses or takes care of high medical costs relating to the child.

The Support Formula

Child support is based on a formula that considers both parents' combined total monthly income prior to any deductions for taxes or other forms of withholding. That figure then determines the child support payment on a pro rata basis. The payment increases with the number of children. However, the payment does not increase in an equal amount per child. The child support guidelines are comparable to federal income tax charts that display similar increases with the income of the parents and the number of children.

The child support calculation also considers day care expenses and health insurance costs related to the children. If the parent paying child support also pays for health insurance, that parent receives a credit against child support for the payment of that premium.

Appendices D-F at the end of this book contain the charts and forms necessary to calculate the amount of child support that must be paid by a parent with as many as six children. Appendix D is used to estimate child support expenses, giving parents a true picture of the costs of raising a child. Appendix E is a State of Alabama Child Support Obligation Income Affidavit (CS-41,-42,-43, and -47), which must be executed by each parent. Appendix F is the state's schedule of basic child support obligations under varied levels of combined monthly gross income for the parents. These forms help you estimate the amount of child support that may be applicable in your case. There are many variables in these calculations, so it is strongly suggested that you consult your attorney concerning how the guidelines apply to your case and what the exact numbers may be.

Alabama Child Support Guidelines are capped at a $10,000 combined monthly income. In cases where the total monthly income exceeds this amount, the guidelines do not apply and child support is based on the needs of the children. This can be a contentious argument, since there are few criteria for determining the needs of children and the specific calculations for child support in high-income cases. This is completed on a case-by-case basis, and many times these cases result in litigation. There have been child support awards of $6,000 to $10,000 a month in certain cases, but there is almost always a dispute over the difference between the needs and wants of the children. Typically, the court tries to maintain a lifestyle similar to what the children enjoyed during the marriage. If the children of a wealthy household have always had access to expensive extracurricular activities, the court will consider those expenses.

The child support guidelines contain certain limitations on child care costs. You may be limited to the Alabama Department of Human Resources' recommended guidelines for day care expenses. If so, these numbers may be considerably less than the cost of private child care, and the custodial parent may be forced to bear the majority of this expense unless there is a variation in the agreement with the noncustodial parent.

An unemployed parent may not be required to pay child support until he or she is once again employed. The court can calculate income based on earning potential for the unemployed spouse. If a payor parent is self-employed, it is often difficult to estimate that party's true income. Many self-employed people receive income in cash, and this income is difficult to prove in a contested divorce. If you are involved in a divorce with a self-employed person, financial records and other documentation are extremely important and valuable in proving your case. Sometimes, the lawyer will look at consumption rather than income and illustrate to the court the purchases made by the spouse, despite the declared income. For example, a person who pays a $1,500 monthly mortgage, $500 car payment, $1,000 in credit card bills, $800 for taxes and insurance, plus an indeterminate amount for groceries and incidentals could only get by on a $2,500 per month draw if he or she was employed as a magician. Some dogs, like this one, don't hunt, and most judges instantly recognize the fact.

Withholding Child Support

You can have child support withheld directly from your spouse's paycheck in Alabama through an income withholding order, if the payor spouse lives in the state or the employer does business here. Most jurisdictions require that an income withholding order be entered automatically, unless the parties can reach an alternate arrangement, with the noncustodial spouse paying the custodial spouse directly. These orders are becoming the norm in many cases. They simplify payments and no longer reflect negatively on the paying spouse.

You may enter an income withholding order in the court clerk's office at the time of the divorce, but stipulate that it is not served upon the paying spouse's employer until he or she becomes delinquent in child support by more than 30 days. If you are concerned that your soon-to-be ex will not pay child support without some force being applied, it is much simpler to address this issue at the time of divorce than to enforce an income withholding order in the future.

Post-Majority College Support

In most cases, child support must be paid until children reach 19 years of age, the age of majority in Alabama, unless the children marry or become self-supporting. Beyond that age, children can only receive child support for payment of specific college and other education-related expenses. If at all possible, the payment of college expenses should be addressed in the settlement agreement. Most settlement agreements specify that one parent will pay these expenses, or the parties will divide them on some pro rata basis. Eligible expenses include tuition, books and room and board. The parties may agree to pay other items such as a weekly allowance, entertainment fees, fraternity and sorority expenses, and transportation to and from school, but courts will rarely order these expenses to be paid. Usually, scholarships are credited against these expenses and regular child support is discontinued when the parent pays these specific expenses.

The court usually will not force a parent to pay private university tuition without a prior agreement between the parties. Costs for most private colleges can total as much as double the amount for public schools. If, for example, a child wants to attend a private university, the agreement should specify the anticipated school or level of support to avoid any confusion in the future. Vanderbilt or Duke may be the child's preferred choices, but the paying parent may argue that community college is a better alternative.

The college obligation usually continues until each child receives his or her undergraduate degree, but no longer than a specified time period from the date he or she graduates from high school. Usually, the child must maintain an overall "C" average or better and be on track toward obtaining a college degree within the specified time period. Most parents request access to the child's grades and academic standing.

If a parent will not agree to the payment of college expenses at the time of settlement, or if the children have not reached high school at the time of the divorce, the court may reserve the issue of college support in the settlement agreement. This gives the custodial parent the right to come back to court and ask for the payment of these expenses in the future. A formal request must be made to the court before the child reaches age 19, or it is forever waived. If this is a contested issue, the court will look to the actual expenses of the college education and the child's scholastic aptitude for college. Rarely will the court force a parent to pay for college for a student who does poorly in school. And you must realize that when the issue of college support is reserved, it is difficult to plan for this major expense in the future and additional attorney's fees will be required to implement the request.

College support after the divorce is a hotly contested issue with serious constitutional undertones. I think all parents should be required to pay for college for their children. However, it is surely unconstitutional that a child of an intact, happy marriage cannot require the parents to pay for college, whereas a child of a divorce can compel payment of college tuition. There are many concerns affecting the decision to pay for college: the behavior and attitude of the child, the child's scholastic aptitude and the relationship of the child with the parent. Furthermore, if parents are ordered to pay for college and fail to comply, they can be put in jail for contempt. This is an issue that has been declared unconstitutional in many states. At this writing, it is up for review in Alabama.

I was confronted by the woman who, at the close of the case, asked me why I would not make her unemployed, alcoholic husband get a job. I said to her, "How can you expect me to do in one trial what you couldn't accomplish in 20 years?"

An Alabama Circuit Court Judge

CHAPTER THIRTEEN

Domestic Violence: Dirty Little Secret That's Not So Small Anymore

THE U.S. DEPARTMENT OF JUSTICE reports that at least 960,000 (and as many as three million) women are victims of domestic violence each year in this country. Intimate partner violence is the number one cause of injury to women — more than automobile accidents, rapes and muggings combined. You can look at divorce as an outlet for victims of domestic violence who need to escape by leaving the marriage. Victims of domestic violence should immediately seek help to protect yourselves and your children. One of the statistical realities is that if men will batter wives and girlfriends, they will often make victims of the kids. To get help, you must take that first difficult step and admit to an abusive relationship. If your spouse does any of the following things, you may need to seek professional help.

Does your spouse hit, kick or strike you?
Does your spouse threaten you with weapons?

Does your spouse scream at you or threaten you?
Does your spouse break items throughout the house?
Does your spouse force sex?
Does your spouse threaten to harm you if you leave?

If your spouse does any of these things, take immediate action to protect yourself. You can begin by seeking the help of professionals who can explain your options. If you are in immediate danger, leave now. If necessary, stay with other family members, friends or in a shelter until you can obtain relief through the court. If you have to leave due to an abusive situation, make every effort to take your children with you. If this is an issue in your case, seek legal help before taking further action.

Involve the Police

If the situation warrants, call the police, who can intervene on your behalf. If you cannot call the police before you leave, call them from a safe location, as soon as possible. If the police believe sufficient evidence exists, they can arrest your spouse on the scene. The police may, however, ask you to swear out a warrant pressing charges against him. This process usually involves you swearing out a warrant with a magistrate in the jurisdiction where the abuse took place. Once a warrant has been issued, the police will arrest your spouse and the case will be set for trial. This can be a lengthy and involved process. If it is a first offense, the court may recommend counseling rather than jail time. Start to establish a history of this type of behavior so the court will be compelled to put your spouse in jail for repeated incidents. Statistics show that a woman is abused in the U.S. every 15 seconds. If you are in this type of situation, you need to seek help immediately, before it escalates to a potentially fatal situation. Too many times, people have looked the other way and discounted the violent potential of people and situations, only to witness the horrible aftermath of their inaction played out in their lives and the lives of their children.

When A Child is Abused

The most emotional type of case we deal with involves child abuse. This type of case usually involves a young child who has been physically or sexually abused by a parent, close family member or friend. These cases require immediate action and usually involve facts that increase in severity as the case proceeds and more information becomes available. Do not make the mistake of thinking this type of abuse cannot happen to your child. Remember that child abuse can occur within any racial, ethnic, religious or economic group. We have represented parents from all economic and social backgrounds, and I firmly believe that child abuse can occur in even the wealthiest of families. Rich people simply have the resources to cover up abuse.

I will not represent a parent who has admitted abuse or been shown to have abused their child. That is my personal policy. I do not want to participate in this type of case unless I am on the side of the parent protecting the child. It saddens me that some people feel compelled to do these horrid things to children, but I have little sympathy for the mental state of the abuser. I'm too busy supplying resources that will help defenseless children overcome the wrath brought down on them by those who abuse them.

One of the best resources to help abused children is a member institution of the Alabama Network of Children's Advocacy

Centers, Inc. These centers bring together the therapeutic and law enforcement services of public and private agencies to support abused children and apprehend their perpetrators. There are 24 children's advocacy centers throughout the state, and a list of those institutions can be found in Appendix L at the end of this book.

Dealing With Fraudulent Allegations

Of course, there is another side to charges of child sexual abuse. The near hysteria generated over spousal and child abuse has caused a dramatic increase in fraudulent allegations by opposing parties trying to affect the outcome of cases. It's sad to see parents lie about physical or sexual abuse immediately after a divorce complaint is filed. You can often tell, from the timing of events, which charges have merit. It amazes me when a parent who never took any action before the divorce claims child abuse in the aftermath. With those charges, everyone makes a great effort to keep the "abusive spouse" away from the children. In fact, so many parents have lied about this type of abuse that they have created a much higher burden of proof for legitimate abuse cases. There is now a presumption that the other spouse is lying in many of these cases.

The Alabama Department of Human Resources is the agency empowered to investigate neglect or child abuse charges. Most of these child abuse or neglect reports originate with school teachers and counselors, followed by law enforcement officials, relatives, parents, social service agency employees, neighbors, hospital personnel, mental health workers and physicians. DHR has the power to remove the child from the home immediately. The department's goal, however, is to keep the child with one of the parents rather than removing the child from the home. In most cases, the agency will make every effort to keep the child with a family member.

The Exchange Club of Birmingham, which also works with abused kids, reports that three children die and 483 children are seriously harmed or disabled every day from child abuse and neglect in the United States. Child abuse victims can eventually overcome the scars of their abuse, but this may require extensive counseling and concentrated efforts on the parent's behalf. A list of private therapists who deal with abuse in Alabama is included in Appendix L.

Documenting Abuse

If you believe your child may be the victim of child abuse, document the abuse with sound medical evidence, including doctor's reports and photographs. There is no piece of evidence more damaging during a divorce trial than a photograph of the bruised face of a child. Immediately seek professional legal and medical help to ensure that your child receives the necessary protection he or she deserves. Your pediatrician is a great source of immediate help and can direct you to other professional help. Professionals who believe child abuse is indicated have a duty to report the abuse to the appropriate agency and spur that agency to action. Once the action begins, you may not be able to stop it. You need to make all necessary preparations to deal with the situation, including seeking sound legal advice concerning a divorce.

*But in this world nothing can
be said to be certain,
except death and taxes.*

Benjamin Franklin

CHAPTER FOURTEEN

Don't Overlook Income Taxes and Insurance

AN INCOME TAX LIABILITY may come back to haunt you if you don't include it in the settlement agreement. You may not even know about the liability. This happens because you often have to file individual returns for the year of the divorce. You don't get to see the complete tax situation as you would if filing a joint return. Consult with your accountant about any tax consequences related to your divorce. If you don't have an accountant, your lawyer can recommend an individual who can quickly evaluate the impact of your agreement from a tax standpoint. At the very least, determine how to divide any liability or refund for the year and address that in the settlement agreement.

Tax Liability

Sometimes, you must deal with a tax liability or refund from a previous year. Language in the settlement agreement should specify who is responsible for any deficiency assessment for liabilities in prior years. Many spouses are not aware of the information contained in the tax returns and are surprised if a deficiency or audit arises after the divorce.

Your agreement should also tell who receives the tax exemptions for the children. The custodial parent usually is awarded these exemptions, since the child support guidelines are calculated with that in mind. However, the parties may agree to divide or split the exemptions, due to other factors related to the settlement. For example, if one spouse is not working and has little income, and the other is working at a higher income, the tax exemptions may benefit the spouse with the higher income much more than the spouse who is working for a minimal amount. If the custodial parent determines that he or she does not really need the tax exemptions, trading them for some other asset may make sense for both parties. The custodial parent must execute Internal Revenue Service form 8332 (see Appendix G) if he or she decides to release the claim to the exemptions.

"This form waives the right to claim the child and can waive that right to the noncustodial parent for one or all years and should be sent with the tax return," says William B. Stapp, Certified Public Accountant for the accounting firm of Stapp and Stapp, PC in Selma. "The IRS doesn't want to get into the situation where they ask 'Who wants them this year?' Consult with your accountant and lawyer before you hand over any tax exemptions."

Health Insurance for the Children

One parent usually is required to provide and maintain hospital and major medical insurance for a minor child until that child reaches age 19. The settlement agreement should also address which party is responsible for medical expenses not covered by health insurance. One spouse can be fully responsible for these expenses or the parties may agree to split these amounts in some fashion. Typical expenses include reasonable charges for doctor, hospital, prescription drugs, optical, dental, orthodontic or other medically-related charges. Don't gloss over this issue, because medical expenses associated with children can be monumental. If a child is diagnosed with a major illness such as leukemia, these expenses can be devastating.

If a child attends college, the agreement should also indicate if the coverage continues until the child graduates. If no health insurance coverage is available to either spouse, it may be difficult to force one or the other to obtain coverage. If a spouse is unemployed, benefits such as health insurance may also be difficult to obtain after the divorce.

Health Insurance for the Spouse

In most cases, health insurance plans will not allow a spouse to continue to provide coverage for his or her ex. A spouse, therefore, must look at other options.

First, a spouse may obtain coverage through his or her own employer. This often is the cheapest solution to this problem.

Second option: a spouse may continue health insurance coverage through the other spouse's insurance plan under the COBRA plan, at least for a limited time. COBRA, the Consolidated Omnibus Budget Reconciliation Act of 1985, is a federal law that allows someone to continue coverage under a plan that had insured the person before he or she became ineligible for it. The premiums associated with COBRA coverage are often higher than the previous payments through the employer. This is especially true in cases where the employer's plan paid all or a portion of that person's premium. Once it goes into COBRA, you are responsible for the entire premium plus plus a 10 to 20% administration fee.

Each spouse should confirm that this type of coverage is available before the final resolution of the case. The settlement agreement should also address who pays the premiums.

If all else fails, the spouse can obtain coverage through an independent source. The settlement agreement can specify that the other spouse must pay the premiums for a specified period of time. However, this is a difficult provision to obtain in a divorce, and it may be extremely difficult to be successful at trial with such a request.

Most individual insurance policies do not cover pre-existing conditions. If you have a major health condition such as cancer or a heart condition, the new policy probably will not cover the new insurance after the divorce. You may require alimony due to the costs associated with medical conditions such as cancer and other major illnesses, as well as the limitations those illnesses place on your ability to work. As a result, health conditions may be a disputed issue in your divorce. For example, the husband of an ill woman may argue that she is not really sick, but is simply making up an illness to get sympathy. To refute this claim, the wife's attorney may have to secure a physician to testify to the wife's condition and its impact on her ability to work. Hiring a doctor to come to court and testify is an expensive proposition. A client in this instance may significantly reduce the cost by rounding up the medical records related to the condition for the lawyer to review. Otherwise, the lawyer will have to subpoena the medical records at a considerable expense. Make certain there is a large amount of money at stake to make the investment worthwhile.

Protect Your Payments With Life Insurance

If one side in a divorce owes money to the other after the divorce is final, either through child support or some type of spousal payments, it only stands to reason that the payor spouse would be required to provide life insurance coverage on himself, for a certain time period, with the children or the ex-spouse as beneficiary. The settlement agreement should specify the amount of the insurance and the term needed to cover the indebtedness.

The obligated spouse should not be allowed to modify the life insurance policies or diminish the value of the life insurance in any way, either by loan, pledge, assignment or reduction. If children are involved, one spouse may require that a trust be established for the life insurance proceeds. Under such a trust, the payor spouse specifies a trustee — often the former spouse or family member — to use the life insurance proceeds for the benefit of each child. When each child reaches a specified age, usually 21, the trustee may be required to distribute a percentage of the proceeds of the trust to the child.

The next time I think about getting married, instead I'll just find a woman who hates me and buy her a house.

Lewis Grizzard

CHAPTER FIFTEEN

Who Gets the House?

HOW MANY PEOPLE BUY MORE HOME than they can afford? Lending institution practices allow people to borrow the maximum amount of money that they, as a couple, can barely afford to repay. Then when the couple divorces and suddenly they are trying to pay for two separate households, along with child support payments, what was once a tight squeeze becomes impossible.

Do You Really Want It?

Dealing with who gets the house after a divorce can become an emotional roller coaster ride. You or your spouse, or both, may believe you have to stay in the house until bad memories hit and you no longer want to live there. Whether you want to keep the house, of course, is irrelevant if you can't make the payments. With all of these issues at hand, the marital residence is often one of the biggest concerns in a property settlement. A good matrimonial law attorney will examine your financial ability to maintain the residence before recommending how to handle the situation. This generally involves looking at your income along with any potential child support or alimony payments and debts.

The chart of living expenses in Appendix B will prove very beneficial in determining whether or not you can afford to keep the residence. Completing this form may lead to a stark realization about the consequences of the divorce, but it is much better to know what's possible ahead of time than to fight for two years to get a house you can't afford.

Once you determine whether to keep the residence, several options are available, including the following:

- Sell the home and divide the equity
- Transfer the home to the other spouse
- Transfer the home to the other spouse for a certain number of years and then sell it
- Deed the home to one side with a cash payment for the equity

Sell the Home and Divide the Equity

If you decide to sell the residence immediately, the settlement agreement should state that it will be sold and the proceeds divided as you agree. One party may receive all of the equity or you may divide as you deem fit. The property should be appraised and placed on the market for the appraisal amount. In the event that you and your ex can't agree upon an appraised value, each of you may select an independent appraiser to value the property. These two independent appraisers can select a third appraiser who will agree on the value of the residence.

After the house is appraised, you should agree on an agent to sell the home. If you can't agree on an agent, each of you can select an agent who will confer and choose a third person to serve as the agent for both parties. Until the real estate sells, your agreement should specify who pays the mortgage payment, taxes, insurance and utilities. The agreement should also require the party living in the home to provide routine maintenance and upkeep. The responsibility for paying the cost of minimal repairs, such as structural, heating, cooling, roofing and appliances, should also be addressed.

The cost of necessary repairs or improvements to prepare the house for sale should be deducted from money received for the real estate, unless one party agrees to bear this cost.

The agreement should also specify that when the house is sold, the following items will be deducted from the gross sales price:

- The amount of the mortgage
- The brokerage commission
- Legal fees related to the sale
- Cost of repairs or improvements
- Cost of sale
- Any other related terms of the settlement agreement, such as the payment of another debt

Transfer the Home To the Other Spouse

If you merely transfer your interest to the other party, the agreement should specify that the transferring party conveys all interest in the residence and agrees to execute a warranty or quit claim deed as part of the settlement agreement. The agreement should also specify who is solely responsible for the mortgage indebtedness on the residence.

Keep the Existing Mortgage

If you and your ex originally signed the mortgage papers together, both parties remain liable for it unless you refinance the property. As a result, if your ex defaults on the mortgage, the mortgage company may look to you for payment of the debt, even though you transferred your interest.

"A lot of people are confused by this issue, but it's simple," says Chris Robbins, vice president of First Commercial Bank in Birmingham. "Regardless of the circumstances, the loan note takes precedence over a divorce decree, and this can affect your credit if your former spouse defaults on the loan.

"It's always better to get the debt refinanced and remove your name from the loan," Robbins says. "People often try to get their names off the note, letting their spouse take it over. If the other spouse does not have the credit to take the loan, though, it must remain in both names."

If one spouse does not pay the obligation, it can cause tremendous hardship and difficulties for the other. This may require a court action to either enforce payment of the mortgage or force the sale of the residence.

Regardless of the situation, this mortgage obligation will continue to show up on credit reports and will have to be addressed in future loan applications. Sometimes, you can handle this by showing the creditor a copy of the divorce decree that indicates the other spouse is responsible for the mortgage obligation.

Transfer the Home to the Other Spouse For a Certain Number of Years and Then Sell It

Specify in the settlement agreement that one party has sole use of the home until a certain time, when it will be sold and the equity divided. This option is common when there are young children and the immediate sale of the residence would disrupt their lives. The wife may be awarded the property for several months or years — until the children turn 19, complete college or move out on their own — or the wife remarries.

The settlement agreement must say how long one spouse can use the residence and what events trigger a sale. The agreement must detail who provides routine maintenance and upkeep, as well as payment of the mortgage obligation. If one spouse occupies the home for a long period of time, the parties must decide whether the equity will be capped at its present value or at its value at the time of sale. If one spouse makes all of the payments after the divorce, that party will not want to share the appreciation.

Deed the Home to One Party With A Cash Payment

Under this option, one party pays the other party a specified sum to take over the marital residence. The terms of this payment must be addressed in the settlement agreement, along with the mortgage obligation and the existing mortgage.

Tax Consequences From the Sale of the Home

The tax consequences of selling a home used to be a great consideration in a settlement agreement. To avoid capital gains taxes in the past, you had to reinvest in another home within 18 months to avoid a tax liability. These rules were changed several years ago. Today, an individual can shelter up to $250,000 in profit from the sale of a home without paying capital gains, whether or not you reinvest the money in real estate.

Never marry for money. Ye'll borrow it cheaper.

Scottish Proverb

CHAPTER SIXTEEN

Arguments Over the Toaster Oven

FOR SOME PEOPLE, custody of their children is the most hotly contested issue in a divorce. For others, the hot topics are who gets the Ming Dynasty vase given as a wedding present or the Elvis Presley CDs that belonged to them before the marriage.

Assets Worth the Fight

At some point during the divorce, you will need to divide the following property: marital property acquired by both spouses during the marriage, gifts and inheritances received by both spouses during the marriage, and separate property which each spouse brought into the marriage or purchased with separate assets during the marriage. A multitude of potential assets and associated liabilities should be addressed in the settlement agreement.

These assets may include the following:

- Furniture and furnishings of the residence
- Bank accounts

- Stocks
- Bonds
- Checking accounts
- Savings accounts
- Life insurance
- Retirement plans
- Individual retirement accounts
- 401K plans
- Jewelry
- Automobiles
- Antiques
- Family heirlooms
- Sporting equipment
- Artworks
- China, silver, crystal
- Boats and trailers
- Personal collections such as coins and stamps
- Gun collections
- Business equipment
- Tools
- Yard equipment

In an ideal situation, you will be able to agree on most, if not all, of the property division. If you reach that point, you will need to address the specific division of the property and the responsibility of each party for any debts.

Factors The Court Considers

If the parties cannot agree on a division of property, the court then must undertake the division itself. The judge can consider a wide variety of factors in the division of the property, including the following:

- Which party owns the property
- If the property was owned prior to the marriage
- If the property was purchased during the marriage
- Any contributions to the property by either party, including money and labor
- Length of the marriage
- The parties' respective ages, health, occupations, employability and ability to produce income
- The degree to which a spouse has diminished his or her future earning capacity because of years spent caring for the children
- The opportunity for each spouse to acquire additional capital, assets or income in the future
- What alimony payments will be made
- What each party should equitably receive in the division
- The fault of the parties

You Should Decide

It is in your best interest to work out an amicable division of the personal property, instead of leaving these decisions to the judge. For one thing, you know what property you want. Secondly, you have more time to go into painstaking detail on a property division. A judge, on the other hand, doesn't really want to divide personal property. He will deal with the property division much more quickly, to expedite resolution of the entire case. He doesn't have the time to ruminate over the fact that you are fond of that armoire in the bedroom, or that only you watched the big-screen television.

"Unless there was no other way, I would not want a judge to decide property and custody issues," says one Alabama Circuit Court judge. "Our knowledge of the history and facts of the case is simply too limited. For that reason, I have become a strong advocate of mediation, where the parties can take more time to expand upon a solution than the judge can in a trial setting."

The judge, in fact, will draw a big line somewhere down the list of property. He may split the property evenly, but he may not understand the worth of certain assets and could split the property very unevenly. If one party does not get a particular piece of property, it may be gone forever if the other spouse does not want to trade it for something else. You may have to go to trial over other significant issues, but try your best to work out the personal property issues with your spouse without help from the judge.

Don't get caught up in an ego war over personal property so intense that when all the dust settles, you have paid your lawyer thousands of dollars to successfully fight for only hundreds of dollars worth of property. I remember a horrible custody battle that we tried in court for several days and then nearly resolved, except the settlement talks failed over possession of a Lincoln Towncar. Keep in mind, the custody issue was resolved, but we could not settle the issues concerning this automobile. The parties' true priorities become abundantly clear when this type of situation happens. The car proved to be far more important to the parties than the children.

The following chapter addresses how major personal property issues can be addressed in a settlement agreement, and whether these issues are simple or complicated.

A big case is never simple;
neither is a small one.

Anonymous Divorce Lawyer

CHAPTER SEVENTEEN

Dividing Major Assets of the Marriage

BUSINESSES DON'T EXIST IN A VACUUM. Neither do retirement accounts and other major assets. When people divorce, all assets are integral parts of a couple's net worth and must be divided in an equitable manner. If those assets consist of a home, a closely-held business, several investment and retirement accounts, other pieces of real estate and other items of personal property, the job of dividing the marital estate can be difficult and must be taken as a whole.

If one party receives the business, the judge will often require that other assets go to the party who does not get ownership of the business to offset its value. If only one large asset is available to the couple, the judge may not be able to divide it. In that case, chances are that asset will be sold and the proceeds divided by the judge in some manner.

The theory of equitable division, that governs how assets are divided in an Alabama divorce, requires that marital property be looked at as a whole and divided equitably.

Dividing Personal Property

Personal property generally includes household furniture and furnishings, goods, wares and appliances, along with each individual's clothing, jewelry and personal items. Most settlement agreements specify one of two things about this type of property; either the parties have already divided the personal property and neither party makes any claim to the other's, or the agreement contains a specific list of the property each party is to receive.

If you and your spouse are fairly amicable, this may not be an important issue to address in the settlement agreement. You may be cooperative enough to divide the household property without help from the judge. If you find it impossible to agree on the simplest of issues, such as the division of towels and sheets, the agreement needs to specify every item you receive. When the agreement states that the wife shall receive one-half of the pictures in the residence, it needs to specify exactly which pictures she receives. You may own assets in an odd number that cannot be divided, and you could end up spending more on legal fees to fight over a toaster or a couch than you would replacing that item. You must assess whether the emotional and financial cost of fighting over certain property is worth all the trouble. Many divorce clients later admit that their decisions were based on ego and pride rather than logic, and due to the memories associated with an item, they did not even want that item anymore.

Closely-Held Businesses

Determining how a business will be held and whether you can sell it can be an important feature of a divorce. The settlement agreement needs to detail who receives the business and how it will be managed after the divorce. If one party receives the business, you need to specify if the other spouse is obligated for any business debts or taxes now or in the future. If the business is successful, an independent accounting of the books and records of the business may be needed to determine its true value.

More games are played over the value of a family business than any other asset in a divorce. The person running the business wants to attach the lowest possible value to the business, because often half of the appraised value must go to the other party. He or she may contend that the market is soft, sales are suffering and those new initiatives just aren't working.

The person who does not run the company only sees an unbroken string of successful years and a good living for the family. This person wants the judge to accept the highest possible value for the company, so that he or she can lay claim to a greater share of the other marital assets.

I recall one owner who had a very successful business at issue in a hotly contested case. He claimed the business was worth just $20,000. We knew during the trial that the business was worth many times more than that. We offered to purchase the business for $40,000, and have a cashier's check to him within three hours. The owner, of course, would not sell the business at twice the value he placed on the business because he said a lot of factors go into valuing a business, and he felt its potential was there. So much for his creative accounting. Once he refused to take the bait at twice the claimed value of the business, he was forced to get realistic about its true value. The overall settlement was drastically affected when the business was proven to be worth significantly more money than the owner's original evaluation.

Retirement Accounts

Retirement benefits are often the largest marital assets of the parties, and should be considered before any determination is made on the fairness of the overall settlement agreement. You may be entitled to a share of your spouse's retirement plan in a property division and should consider accepting part of the plan rather than other assets.

In many long-term marriages, the husband often wants his retirement money and the wife wants the house. But a retirement plan may be several times more valuable than the equity in the marital residence. A woman may have an emotional attachment to the home, but she may be making a mistake if she accepts it.

You should make every effort to obtain a recent statement for the retirement plan, showing its present value as well as future values. If no one will give you this information, a lawyer can obtain it from the account manager through the discovery process.

"When looking at retirement plans at the time of a divorce, I always advise people to keep an eye out for any large distribution from the accounts," says Zach Ivey, a financial planner for First Financial in Birmingham. "Spouses have a tendency to take money out of their retirement plans before filing for a divorce. It's easy to track these distributions, since all of them are documented in the account paperwork."

In addition to splitting the account, you should look at the survivor benefits under the retirement plan. Ivey says that survivor benefits applicable in the event of the spouse's death may also provide security for a spouse and should be addressed in the settlement agreement. The agreement should state that benefits cannot be assigned or reduced in any fashion. If this is an issue in your divorce, it may be wise to spend some time verifying the actual values of the retirement plan and tax complications with your lawyer and your accountant.

The most effective way to divide a retirement plan is through a Qualified Domestic Relations Order (QDRO), which basically splits the plan into two separate plans. QDROs offer protections to both parties. To the party who receives a share of the other party's plan, the QDRO splits off as much as 50% of the appreciation of the plan that occurred during the marriage without the tax complications associated with dividing the plan prior to maturity. The plan's original owner is also protected from any tax liability from the portion of the plan given to the other party.

Lovers' quarrels are not generally about money. Divorce cases generally are.

Mason Cooley

CHAPTER EIGHTEEN

Alimony

A RULE APPLIES TO THE PAYMENT of alimony; recipients praise its fairness, and those making payments think it is a form of cruel and unusual punishment. There are limited circumstances where a spouse is willing to pay a reasonable amount, but those cases are the exception. There is usually debate about the amount and length of the term of the alimony payment. The following discussion summarizes alimony in its basic forms and the factors the court considers.

Rehabilitative Alimony

This form of alimony is designed to help a spouse recover financially after the divorce and is payable for only a short period of time. Rehabilitative alimony is appropriate for a spouse who has not worked in several years or is working but needs time to recover from the financial impact of the divorce. The goal of rehabilitative alimony is to rehabilitate the spouse over a specified period of time.

Alimony in Gross

Another alimony option consists of one spouse paying a lump sum to the other spouse as part of the property settlement. This payment is usually characterized as alimony in gross, and the settlement agreement should specify the amount and terms of the payment. Alimony in gross may be dischargeable in bankruptcy, and any provisions in this area should be closely examined with your lawyer. Alimony in gross cannot be modified, even if circumstances change.

Periodic Alimony

Periodic alimony generally is awarded in longer-term marriages (more than 10 years) and is valid until the spouse remarries, dies or cohabitates with another individual. On occasion, periodic alimony can be awarded in some short-term marriages as well. There are misconceptions concerning periodic alimony. Many divorcing people believe they are entitled to receive periodic alimony regardless of the length of the marriage, the parties' financial resources or the fault of the parties. But the courts consider numerous aspects of the case when making a periodic alimony award, including the parties' financial resources, which can be the greatest determining factor.

If the debts and obligations of the parties result in a negative cash flow, the court may not award a substantial amount of money. At the same time, the court may award considerable periodic alimony in long- and short-term marriages where the payor spouse's fault caused the breakup of the marriage. In those cases, the value of the alimony award may be from several hundred thousand dollars to several million dollars when the payments are valued over the life of the client.

In certain circumstances, periodic alimony can be modified in the future. The receiving spouse can request a modification if his or her needs change or the resources of the paying party increase. The modification issue can provide a tremendous safety net for the receiving spouse, but also can be a tremendous trap for the paying spouse. You may pay all the periodic alimony ordered, only to discover that your ex-spouse has asked for an extension. Recently, I represented a man who was shocked to learn that his ex-wife filed a petition to extend the alimony he had been paying for 10 years. In the original divorce, the husband gave the wife most of their assets in consideration for paying alimony for only 10 years. The wife requested five years, but the husband extended it to make sure she had more than enough time to get on her feet. During the 10-year period, the husband's income drastically decreased due to changes in the economy, but he continued to make the large alimony payments at a personal sacrifice to himself. With one month remaining, his former wife filed a petition to extend the alimony, alleging she still needed the money. After a lengthy court battle, he eventually succeeded in denying her effort to extend the alimony.

Whether the alimony can be modified rests largely with the specific language in the agreement, and the facts and circumstances of each case. Address the issue of future alimony modification in the settlement agreement.

Periodic alimony is taxable income to the receiving spouse and is deductible to the paying spouse. Meet with your accountant to determine the tax consequences of any periodic alimony award before you can properly evaluate the true value of the payment.

Factors Considered by the Court In Making an Award of Alimony

When determining an appropriate alimony award, the court normally considers the following factors:

- The apportionment of property under the settlement agreement
- The parties' financial resources
- The length of the marriage
- The respective age, health, occupation, employability, and trainability of the parties
- The degree to which one spouse has diminished his or her future earning capacity or education because of years spent caring for children or serving as a homemaker
- Standard of living during the marriage
- Tax consequences of the awarding of alimony
- The fault of the parties

Tax and Bankruptcy Consequences Of Alimony

Alimony payments create specific tax consequences in a divorce, depending on the type of alimony a party receives. In most circumstances, rehabilitative alimony in gross is nontaxable to the receiving spouse and nondeductible to the paying spouse. Periodic alimony, on the other hand, is taxable to the receiving spouse and deductible to the paying spouse. These tax consequences may have a significant effect on the actual value of the award and the cost of the award to the paying spouse. Divorcing couples should consult with their accountants when evaluating the options related to alimony.

The type of alimony you decide upon and how it is dealt with in your agreement can also be affected if you or your ex are contemplating bankruptcy. Federal bankruptcy laws have specific applications for alimony payments. Certain forms of alimony in gross may be discharged in a future bankruptcy action, leaving the recipient spouse with nothing. Periodic alimony, on the other hand, is generally not dischargeable in bankruptcy. If you think your spouse might file bankruptcy to avoid these payments, inform your attorney because the terms of the settlement agreement may drastically affect your rights. Certain language in your settlement agreement may prevent your spouse from avoiding payment of a large amount of past due alimony.

The fail-safe way to protect yourself from losing money to your ex in a bankruptcy is to require, in the settlement agreement, that he or she provide additional security against loss. This may mean giving you a lien against a piece of real property or another valuable asset. Make certain the property does not have any encumbrances on it when you accept the lien, and be sure you can locate and repossess the property if your spouse tries to bankrupt the debt.

Fairness occurs only when you divide all the property among the parties and throw the debts into the sea.

Anonymous

CHAPTER NINETEEN

Apportioning Debt

NOW FOR THE DEBTS, those nagging and pitiful roadblocks to everyday happiness and killer of many a divorce settlement. No one wants to pay the debts a family accumulates over time, especially if they are unsecured and the joy you got from whatever you purchased is long gone.

You must address the payment of debts in the settlement agreement, or they may come back to haunt you or your spouse. The agreement should specify debts each party must pay after the divorce. Once your spouse accepts that these are his or her debts, and you are not responsible for them, you should be indemnified from any expense resulting from the indebtedness, including any attorney's fee for enforcement of the indemnification.

Which Debts Are Whose?

Perhaps the best illustration of the need to be specific about debts is an agreement a woman brought to me several years ago, after she signed it. The agreement stated that "the parties have certain debts and the wife shall pay two of the debts and the husband shall pay two of the debts." Only it didn't specify which two debts each party was supposed to pay! Because of its ambiguity, this agreement is very difficult to enforce, since the court cannot interpret the specific debts from the vague terms.

Pay Off Debts In Your Name

The problem of apportioning debt is confounded by the fact that even though you may be responsible for a certain debt in the settlement agreement, if you don't pay for it the creditor will often go after the other party. This is almost always true if both spouses signed the note creating the indebtedness.

Pay off as many debts as possible, especially those you and your ex signed together. You should also cancel accounts when you can or convert them into the name of one spouse, if the creditor will allow it. If your ex is responsible for a debt and doesn't pay it as ordered, about all you can do is take him or her to court on a contempt action. It may also be appropriate to specify that certain debts be refinanced within a specific time period to remove the spouse from any obligation.

Judges don't look favorably at a spouse who generates a large number of charges on joint credit cards immediately before separating for divorce. As a result, you need to substantiate any recent charges as reasonable and appropriate.

Factors Considered in Apportioning Debt

When addressing responsibility for the marital debts, the court will consider a variety of factors, including the following:

- Whose name the debt is in
- The purpose of the debt
- Who is retaining the asset related to the debt
- Financial resources of the parties
- Any agreement between the parties concerning the debts
- The overall apportionment of property under the settlement agreement
- The length of the marriage
- The fault of the parties

When meeting with your attorney, provide a list of all of the debts from the marriage, including a breakdown of debts incurred by each party or jointly. In addition, provide a detailed list of purchases made to account for the debts, and the current status of those assets. This information should also include the name and address of the creditors, as well as the account numbers.

O'er lawyers fingers, who straight dream on fees;

Shakespeare

CHAPTER TWENTY

Attorney's Fees: Paying For Services Rendered

THE EFFORT BY DIVORCE COURTS across the nation to become more gender neutral has hampered the ability of the less documented spouse to retain competent counsel. In most marriages, one spouse pays the bills, keeps records and retains more cash. That spouse is more documented than the spouse who does not handle the money. That was true in past times, and it's still true today. But the courts want to treat men and women of every marriage the same.

Depending on the facts of your case, you may or may not have to pay your own attorney's fees. Any settlement agreement needs to address who is responsible for payment of the attorney's fees. In most cases, the agreement will either state that parties pay their own attorney's fees, or that one party pays all or part of the other party's fees up to a specified amount, or that the fees are equally divided between the parties. In a contested divorce, an award of attorney's fees by the court is discretionary and depends on the overall terms of the property settlement.

Usually, Each Client Pays

Because of this move toward gender neutrality, most fee agreements place the ultimate responsibility for payment of the fees with each party. If fees are not awarded by the court, or the opposing spouse refuses to pay the awarded fees, the attorney will seek payment of the fees from his or her client. The court may only award a portion of the fees, leaving the client to pay the remaining balance. This court award is usually based upon the overall property award made by the court and not on the court's opinion as to the value of the legal services.

A Good Bargaining Chip

Few divorcing people volunteer to pay the other spouse's attorney's fee. Let's face it: many people would compare this to paying someone to rob you, and they might be willing to make a financially questionable deal to avoid handing over that check to the other lawyer. You, on the other hand, should think of attorney's fees as you would a bank account or other asset or liability in the divorce. As a strategy, you might agree to pay your own attorney's fees in exchange for a larger share of a bank account or asset. Your spouse may be willing to give you a $20,000 bank account, for instance, but not $5,000 to pay the attorney who negotiated the deal for you. You would be better served to take the bank account and pay your own attorney's fees. Don't get hung up on the need to have these fees paid for you.

Divorce puts you on the edge of sanity.

Abigail Trafford

CHAPTER TWENTY-ONE

The Miscellany of Divorce

DID YOU KNOW THAT FOR A WOMAN to reclaim her maiden name, she must obtain a court order? Many wives want to return to their maiden name after a divorce. If so, the settlement agreement should specify that the wife may reclaim her former name. No matter when this is done, it requires the completion of additional legal forms. It is simpler to handle this at the time of the divorce by requesting that the judge grant her the use of her former name in the settlement agreement. If there are still young children in the family, many wives do not change their names in an effort to avoid confusion, and some judges refuse to grant the name change for the benefit of those children.

Warranties

The settlement agreement also should specify that both parties stipulate that the agreement makes fair and equitable provisions for the distribution of their property, and that both parties have full knowledge of and have made full disclosure of all separate marital assets. Specify that both parties are voluntarily executing the agreement and are free of any undue influence or duress other than the normal stresses of divorce.

The agreement should state that the settlement contains the entire understanding and agreement between the parties, that it is a full and complete settlement, and that there are no representations, warranties, covenants or undertakings other than those expressly set forth in the agreement.

The agreement should also say that obligations cannot be discharged under the federal bankruptcy code. This provision may not fully exempt certain obligations in the bankruptcy court, but it may help the party attempting to enforce the obligation in divorce court because it shows the intent of the parties.

Necessary Documents

The settlement agreement should compel each party to execute and deliver all documents necessary to complete the agreement. For example, certain documents such as car titles or insurance forms may need to be signed well after the divorce is final. It should be a matter of common sense that the parties agree on signing basic documents. Because of the emotions present during and after a divorce, though, if it is not specified in the agreement, many parties will feel they do not have to do it.

Non-Compliance

The agreement should state that if either party incurs any expense as a result of the breach of any portion of the settlement agreement by the other party, the court shall award reasonable attorney's fees and other expenses to the nondefaulting party. While this provision may not be enforceable in every instance, it usually provides leverage to the party attempting to enforce a provision of the agreement in the future.

Modification

Any modification or waiver of any provision of the settlement agreement should only be effective if made in writing, executed with the same formality as the settlement agreement and approved by the court. This is important because sometimes a party will claim that "she told me it was okay not to pay the child support."

Litigation is a machine which
you go into as a pig
and come out as a sausage.

Ambrose Bierce

CHAPTER TWENTY-TWO

Preparing for Trial

FOR MANY PEOPLE, a divorce is the only experience they will ever have in a courthouse. Besides adding to the stress related to going through a divorce, the courthouse provides a very sobering experience for many people. I would highly recommend that anyone going through a litigated divorce visit the courthouse to observe a trial before attending your own hearing. It is unsettling for many litigants who arrive at a crowded courthouse on the day of a hearing to adjust to the legal process on such short notice. Your lawyer should be able to direct you to the appropriate courthouse beforehand, so that you can view a similar hearing. Study your particular judge's demeanor, as well as the process itself. Simply knowing where the courthouse is located and where the restrooms and vending machines are in the building will make your experience a little easier.

When you visit the courthouse, take a pen and paper so you can write down any questions you have for your lawyer. You may hear the judge make a statement to one of the other lawyers that you think is directly relevant to your case. You need to review this information with your lawyer prior to trial.

Makeup of the Court System

In Alabama, almost all family, divorce and child-related matters are handled by the district and circuit courts. The district courts hear all juvenile cases or those involving illegitimate children. The circuit court judges usually preside over divorce cases.

Judges hear virtually all cases involving divorce and post-divorce modifications. In the major cities of our state, certain courts are designated to hear only family issues involving juveniles. In Jefferson County, for instance, three judges hear all divorce cases in the circuit court. Two judges hear all family court matters that involve juveniles and illegitimate children in the district courts.

The system works differently outside the major cities. Circuit court judges hear a variety of cases, from divorce to criminal cases to other civil suits. It is critically important to know the day-to-day experience of the judge in your case.

Before attending a trial, you and your lawyer should review the relevant facts in your case. Each hearing will affect the final outcome, and the two of you should communicate about your case. Your lawyer should meet with you before any hearing. He or she should take you through the steps and explain the relevant issues that will need to be addressed in the courtroom.

Preparation for Court

In complicated cases that warrant extensive witness preparation, your lawyer may prepare you for the hearing by asking you questions similar to those he or she will ask you at trial. He or she should also prepare you for the multitude of questions the opposing lawyer might ask. If your lawyer tells you something that you absolutely must address at the hearing, follow his or her advice. Most divorce experts know exactly what relevant information each judge wants and needs to hear in order to make a decision. If your lawyer advises you not to discuss a certain issue, follow his counsel. For example, many people often want the judge to hear each and every detail of their marriage. The lawyer is keenly aware of the judge's limited time and the possibility that the judge will become overwhelmed with irrelevant or repetitive details. If it is not in your best interest to volunteer something, follow your lawyer's advice.

Your lawyer needs to know the facts and details surrounding the marriage, so that he or she can determine the best way to tell your side of the story. As a result, you may not get to tell the judge everything you want. For example, once you have established in court that your spouse has had an adulterous relationship or was abusive to you, your lawyer must determine how many additional details are required. If your lawyer wastes too much of the judge's time listing the same facts over and over, the judge may become annoyed with you. It is much smarter to move on and avoid giving the opposing party an additional opportunity to rehabilitate his or her testimony. When you testify at trial and the other side asks you questions, you are often limited in your responses. If the other side asks you a "yes or no" question, you should answer that way. Many people want to explain themselves, saying, "Yes, but that is because he...." Your lawyer will give you an opportunity to tell your side of the story, but the other side will limit your testimony to those facts that help them. For example, the other side may ask,

"Have you ever yelled at your children?" In most cases, the answer is "yes," but serious parents will want to explain. You can become upset when the other lawyer cuts you off and says, "Answer the question with yes or no only." In that type of situation, your lawyer will simply give you an opportunity to add to your answer during the time he or she is questioning you.

Practice with your lawyer prior to trial to become familiar with the questions and the type of responses. You should always tell the truth, but there are ways to tell the truth without helping the opposition. Practice sessions will help you, because you will know your lawyer is going to cover the necessary points during the presentation of your case, regardless of the manner in which the other side badgers you during the trial.

What the Judge Needs to Know

You do not have to spew out every distasteful detail about your soon-to-be ex. The judge does not need to know about each and every fight you had, or each and every meal you ever prepared. This does not mean the judge is not interested, but he or she only needs to hear the heart of the case. Judges often say they have heard enough on a particular issue and it is time to move on. Failing to heed the judge's advice can result in an unfavorable ruling, because you have not heeded his or her advice. Even if you do not like the advice, keep in mind that the judge will determine the fate of your case. We tell clients that arguing with the judge is similar to arguing with your former junior high principal. If you were called into the principal's office, arguing with the principal would result in a more stringent punishment. If you argue with the judge, don't be surprised when you get a less-than-favorable result.

Friend:	*How'd your divorce trial go?*
Spouse:	*My lawyer chewed her up.*
Friend:	*Well, what all did you get?*
Spouse:	*Oh, she got everything, but we sure let her have it!*

CHAPTER TWENTY-THREE

Your Day in Court

DIVORCING PEOPLE ARE OFTEN MORE CONCERNED about humiliating the other side on the witness stand than reaching the best possible settlement. Assuming you are unable to settle your case, eventually it will be set for trial on the court's calendar. I say eventually because with so many cases on the docket, you might wait as long as two years after the divorce is filed to finalize the dissolution. This extensive waiting period makes settlement of your divorce case even more preferable.

The first case setting usually is three months or more after the filing of the divorce complaint. A case may be continued several times before it actually reaches trial. The judge may give a continuance when the parties are not ready to try the case or there is a conflict in the attorneys' schedules, in the client's schedule or in the court's docket. Your case may be passed over and continued to a later date if the judge is already in trial on another case, has an immediate issue to address or an older case to hear. A spouse with financial obligations to the other party after the divorce may try to continue the case as long as possible. This either avoids imposing a premature obligation or can force a settlement. Over time, many people become anxious to settle, even accepting an inadequate settlement offer due to the length of time involved in a pending divorce. The inevitable delays should be factored into decisions about settlement of the case and whether the expenses associated with the delays are outweighed by the trial court's potential ruling.

Many spouses fail to believe the other side will actually go to trial. This feeling is usually found in situations where one spouse dominated the other throughout the marriage. In an atmosphere of intimidation, it is often beneficial for the more passive spouse to follow through with the trial. Otherwise, the difficult spouse will continue to harass the more congenial one after the divorce, believing he or she can get away with it.

Plan Your Appearance

When going to court, just like any special occasion, you should dress for success. First impressions are important, but perhaps they are most important in a marital or child custody dispute where a judge is forced to evaluate the credibility of the parties from a limited viewpoint. For men, I generally recommend a suit or nice pair of slacks, white shirt and a tie. A nice dress or suit is appropriate for a woman. If you have any questions about your wardrobe choices, be sure to ask your lawyer or his staff for suggestions. From the moment you leave your house until you enter the courthouse, act in a mature and professional manner. You never know who might see or hear you. You never want to incur the wrath of a judge who hears about one litigant threatening another in the hallway.

At the hearing, be calm and cool, even though deep down you may be quite the opposite. Many cases are settled because one party came to court poker-faced, convincing the other side that he or she was confident and not concerned about going to trial.

Check Your Place on the Court's Docket

The courthouse will be an eye-opening experience for you. Most people have only seen a courthouse on television or in the movies. Real life in court is different from television. For example, 10 to 15 cases may be set on the judge's docket the same day, along with your case. These cases range from very brief motions to other cases set for trial. The parties and witnesses for each case on the docket fill the courtroom. The hallways outside the courtroom are often lined with hard wooden benches filled to capacity with more parties, witnesses and lawyers trying to resolve disputes.

First thing in the morning, the judge calls his docket. This means the judge briefly checks the status of the cases at the top of his list with the attorneys representing the parties. This may involve the attorneys requesting an opportunity to determine if a settlement is possible. It can also involve a range of other issues, from requesting a continuance to asking to speak with the judge about a particular issue in the case that needs clarification before the case can proceed. If the parties are ready for trial, the judge will determine, based on all of the cases he has set that day, which case or cases he will hear that day.

The judge's determination is based on a variety of factors. First, the oldest case usually has priority. If your case was filed with the court clerk three months ago, and another case is 15 months old, the older case has priority. The judge will also evaluate the seriousness of the issues at hand. If there is an emergency issue on the docket — such as an immediate threat of abuse or theft of property — the court usually attempts to resolve these issues, even if it is only a short-term fix.

If 10 to 15 emergencies clog the court's docket the same day as your case, the judge will pick the most pressing and immediate emergency that time will permit him to handle that day. If the judge is already in trial on a case from the previous day, usually he will keep going on that case and continue the others. This is simply the judicial system in action. Your lawyer can't do anything about it and it's just as bothersome to him. Even though you waited three months to get to trial, prepared for the trial with your lawyer and brought your witnesses to the courthouse, your case still may be continued over your lawyer's objections. Recognize in the beginning that your divorce case could be over quite soon, but it could also last for many months, regardless of how badly you want to be done with this.

If extended travel or other hardships make it difficult for you or a witness to come to court on the mere chance that your case will be heard, your lawyer may be able to call the courthouse on the day before your case is set to determine the likelihood that you will go to trial. Some judges will tell the lawyer that he is in trial or has a more pressing case that must get resolved. This helps the lawyer avoid imposing an inconvenience on his client and other witnesses, especially those coming from out of town.

But you might also draw a judge who will require you and your lawyer to be at the courthouse every time the case is set. If your lawyer is an expert in this area, he should be able to tell you whether the judge and his office can help coordinate the scheduling of the trial.

Modulate Your Manner

During the hearing, remain focused on the issue at hand. Sit up straight in your seat and speak clearly. Be polite and remember that the judge is evaluating your responses and your overall demeanor to determine whether you are the evil spouse the other party says you are. Don't be argumentative or hostile with the other side, or answer any questions in a haughty fashion. Remember, your lawyer needs to handle the relevant arguments. The talented trial lawyer on the other side will strive to get you upset on the stand, so that you will lose your temper and show the judge the evil personality that the other side is trying to prove. Human nature makes us all want to respond when we are confronted by another person. Keep in mind that the other side's goal is to affect your focus during the trial. Do not help them achieve their goal.

Answer Questions Truthfully

When opposing counsel at trial questions you, give truthful and accurate answers. Besides the fact that lying on the stand is unethical and illegal, it will ruin your credibility in front of the trial judge if the other side discredits your testimony. If you expect questions about adultery, abuse or other faults in the breakup of the marriage, discuss with your lawyer ahead of time how to handle these issues at trial. While you need to tell the truth in your testimony, you should not offer more information than has been requested by the other side.

It is not your job to prove the other side's case. If the lawyer does not ask the appropriate questions, you may not have to provide certain information. This principle applies to every question you are asked. Once you have answered the question as briefly as possible, be quiet. If you have concerns about how to answer certain questions, discuss them with your lawyer before trial.

Your lawyer will detail a specific plan for handling the case at trial. You need to follow your lawyer's advice and not venture into new territory during the proceedings. Your lawyer will prepare the case based on the information he or she has and how the judge responds to certain information. Even though you may think specific information or evidence is absolutely imperative to clear your good name, it may also annoy the judge and throw your lawyer off course if you venture into new areas. Most divorce lawyers want to know exactly what you plan to say when you are on the stand. Once you discuss the testimony, follow your lawyer's advice about specific issues. It is foolish to not follow your lawyer's advice. Your refusal to follow your lawyer's guidance may cause you to lose your case.

The Final Judgment of Divorce

When your divorce is resolved, the judge will sign a document called a final judgment of divorce. This document divorces the parties and spells out the terms and conditions of the divorce. If the case is settled, the final judgment of divorce will usually adopt the settlement agreement signed by the parties and proclaim it binding on both parties. If the case is tried in court, the final judgment will spell out the court's ruling. Read and understand the terms of the final judgment and the settlement agreement, since you can be held in contempt for not abiding by them. If you have questions or concerns, your lawyer needs to explain all of the terms and conditions of the settlement agreement or final judgment, to ensure that you know your rights and responsibilities. Emotions are at a high level in the courtroom or during settlement of a case. You need to understand all of the conditions of the divorce. For example, many terms may change several times while working out a settlement. People forget certain issues, such as the exact property distribution from the marital residence. Make certain you understand the final terms. You should also put the final judgment away for safekeeping, since you will refer to it in the future as disputes or questions arise about the divorce.

PART 3

What Happens After the Divorce

*Appealing a divorce is like
redrilling a root canal.
If it was done right the first time,
why would that be necessary?*

Anonymous

CHAPTER TWENTY-FOUR

Appealing Your Divorce Decree

DIVORCE ACTIONS IN ALABAMA give you one big juicy bite at the apple of judicial success. Take the largest bite you can during the trial and make the most of it, because you will rarely get another attempt to present your case in court. Your appeal options for relief of the trial court's decisions are limited and rarely succeed, although it may be possible to challenge the court's ruling provided strict time limits are met.

Motion to Set Aside or for a New Trial

You have the right to file a motion to set aside the divorce decree or request a new trial if you are not satisfied with the court's ruling. Under Alabama law, this type of motion generally must be filed within 30 days of the date of the order being contested. These motions usually are not successful, unless the court failed to consider a material fact in evidence, or if the court made a clear and distinct error in its ruling. The trial judge heard the entire trial, is familiar with the case, and can review his notes to determine if an error occurred. Remember that you are asking the judge to admit that he or she made an error in the case. It's difficult for anyone, including a judge, to review and reconsider his or her own behavior and come to a different conclusion. If your motion is not successful, you are then forced to use the appeal process to change the decree.

Time Limits for Appeal

Either party to the divorce has the right to appeal a final judgment. You must file that notice of an appeal within 42 days after the judgment is entered or from the day the post-trial motion is denied, whichever is later.

An appeal is a last-ditch effort to change the divorce decree. It is difficult to win on appeal and there is a presumption in favor of the divorce decree by the trial court, which saw and heard the evidence. The law is specific as to what issues can and cannot be appealed, and the standard of review for such an appeal is stringent. The Alabama Court of Appeals hears the appeal, and it is limited to the evidence you presented at trial. You cannot come into an appeal of your divorce case offering new evidence from witnesses the judge has not heard. Many people are shocked to find their failure to present crucial evidence at trial may ruin their chances for an appeal. To preserve the case you presented at trial, you must have a court reporter record the testimony and any rulings made during the trial in order to have an exact record.

Such an appeal is an expensive legal procedure that can cost significantly more than the divorce itself. The lawyer must write a history of the case for the court of appeals, as well as a history of the testimony at trial. If one lawyer handles the original case and another the appeal, the appellate attorney will have to spend a considerable amount of time getting familiar with the facts of the case. If the appeal is not successful and you decide to petition the Alabama Supreme Court, your lawyer may have to draft additional documents and the costs will continue to rise. That is why it is always more effective to handle the case properly at trial than to rely on the appeal process to remedy an injustice.

Family quarrels are bitter things. They don't go according to any rules. They're not like aches or wounds; they're more like splits in the skin that won't heal because there's not enough material.

F. Scott Fitzgerald

CHAPTER TWENTY-FIVE

The Tough Stuff Begins: Enforcing Your Divorce Decree

ENFORCING A COURT ORDER can be the most trying element of the divorce process, depending on how the parties feel about each other when it's over. The enforcement process can become a game of guerilla warfare, in which one party strikes out against the other and then recedes to find out if the other party will retaliate. This game may involve one party who acts childlike, failing to live up to an agreement or a court order and just daring the other party to come down to his or her level. If children are involved in the divorce, it is unfortunate that they are often the victims most injured by these silly games.

Initiate Contempt Actions

To do away with all the game-playing, often the party being tested has to charge the other with a contempt action. This action against the opposing party can enforce the payments of alimony, child support, attorney's fees, and certain types of financial and property matters, as well as child custody issues. The party filing the contempt action must show that the opposing party failed to comply with a judgment or order of the court. For example, if a party doesn't pay child support, but has worked during the entire time of the contemptuous behavior and chosen to spend the money on other things, that person is guilty of a willful refusal to comply with the divorce decree.

It takes a certain amount of realism on your part to establish the other person's true motivation. For instance, if the opposing party lost a job, through no fault of his or her own, and did not have an income during the time of the missed child support payments, that makes this a different case. Resolution of this issue will depend on the circumstances surrounding the failure to comply with the decree and the party's ability to explain the job loss. Likewise, a parent can also be held in contempt for failing to comply with a visitation schedule or for not returning the child to the custodial parent.

Remember that under a contempt action, often you are asking the court to put the opposing party in jail for failure to comply with the decree. In many cases, this is necessary to show the offending party that the obligation must be met. But do you really want to put your children's mother or father in jail? Certainly this action can diminish your relationship. As a result, you must weigh the seriousness of the contempt against the stark reality of jailing your ex-mate.

Under a contempt ruling, a party may be placed in jail and released by purging the contempt action. For example, the court may order the opposing party to jail until back child support is paid. If the party is financially unable to pay, the court may decide that there is no constructive reason to keep that person in jail. It is amazing, though, how quickly that party, his or her relatives or new spouse can come up with money when jail is an alternative.

Sometimes, you can predict compliance problems with your former spouse prior to the final resolution. If this is a possibility in your case, ask your attorney how to limit the possibility of contempt after your divorce.

Stand Up to Your Ex

Give the opposing party adequate time to comply before filing a contempt action, but don't wait too long to file. Many people wait until they are owed tens of thousands of dollars before filing an action. Even if you are successful with a contempt action, and the ex-spouse resolves to pay the debt, often you will have to accept installment payments over time. Each party should keep detailed records of every support payment received or paid under the divorce decree, to establish a payment history for any future contempt action.

A contempt action should be filed as soon as possible after the party fails to comply. This demonstrates that you demand compliance. Your relationship with the opposing party after the divorce will directly affect your initial actions. If an ex-husband violates the court order without any complaint from the ex-wife, he will probably continue this action in the future. If she will not tolerate missed child support payments or the husband refusing to return the child at a scheduled time, she may be able to limit the contemptuous behavior.

Unfortunately, certain spouses just refuse to abide by the decree and should go to jail for failure to comply. While this is an unfortunate situation, it is critical to send a message to that spouse that compliance with a court order is necessary and required. When people in the courtroom see the sheriff take a party to jail for contempt, great efforts are made to work out problems between the parties.

Criminal lawyers see the worst people at their best.
Divorce lawyers see the best people at their worst.

Thomas B. Concannon, former divorce lawyer

John M. Wood

CHAPTER TWENTY-SIX

Seeking Modification of Your Divorce Decree

A CHANGE IN CIRCUMSTANCES after the original divorce decree was entered may require you to modify certain provisions of that decree. The most common modifications involve child custody, child support, visitation and alimony. The law surrounding a petition to modify is very limited, and you should determine whether a modification is possible on a case-by-case basis.

While modifications to your divorce decree are possible, this should not compel you to take your original case lightly. You should obtain the best possible result in the initial divorce agreement and rely on the modification process only to correct an unforeseen change in circumstances.

Custody Modifications

When the parties do not agree after the divorce about the raising of children, one party may attempt to change the custody arrangement. It is extremely difficult to modify a prior custody award that transfers custody from one parent to the other. A custody modification is one of the most arduous and expensive post-divorce actions. The positive change brought about by the modification must offset the disruptive effect caused by transferring custody. The court doesn't take into consideration what helps a parent. The judge is sworn to rule in the best interest of the child. A parent seeking to modify custody must show the court that the change would promote the child's best interest and that the child is being adversely affected in the present situation. Often, a party will file a custody modification when the actual conflict concerns the other spouse and not whether that spouse has had an impact on the child. The party seeking the modification must show that the child has actually been affected by the change in circumstances.

Simply because the custodial parent has a new boyfriend or girlfriend, for example, does not mean the child's situation has changed for the worse. If the child has not witnessed any elicit or abusive conduct between the parent and the friend, the party asking for the modification may not be able to establish any actual harm. And just because the noncustodial parent's situation has improved, he or she will not automatically receive custody in a modification. For example, many mothers who initially gave up custody due to a personal problem mistakenly believe that they will automatically get custody back as soon as they get their lives back together. Even though the noncustodial parent's situation has improved, it does not mean there is anything wrong with the way the custodial parent has been caring for the child. However, if the noncustodial parent can show serious harm to the child, it may be possible to modify custody. Keep in mind that harm can be in a variety of forms other than abuse. For example, if the custodial parent is driving while intoxicated, with the child in the car, a reasonable argument can be made that the child's safety is in jeopardy.

Modifying custody is a very difficult area of the law that causes extreme tension and emotion between the parties. Many spouses are upset to learn that they may not be able to change the conditions in which their children are living. This is why it is important to address these concerns under the original divorce decree. It is surprising how many parents give an abusive ex either joint custody or substantial visitation rights with a child he or she has abused throughout the marriage. After one parent has granted the abusive parent's visitation, it is very difficult to convince a trial judge during a modification proceeding that the parent's visitation should be limited.

It is possible to modify the custody provisions, but you should be ready for a difficult fight. A custody trial is one of the most difficult and emotionally draining processes you will ever undertake. The legal fees associated with a custody modification can be enormous, and these costs must be weighed in making a decision whether or not to proceed with a modification. If this is an issue in your case, meet with your attorney to determine whether a modification would be in your best interest or if you can work out a different arrangement without going to court. Invest a portion of the potential fees to find out whether you should proceed or if you are not likely to be successful.

Child Support Modifications

If there is an increase or decrease in the income of either party, it may be possible to modify the prior child support award. If the payor spouse's income has significantly increased, the child support payment should probably increase. At the same time, if the payor spouse has lost his job or had his income significantly decreased, that spouse may be entitled to a reduction in child support. Many parents are shocked to find out that their child support payment is going up several hundred dollars or more due to changes in the child support guidelines.

It is also common to modify the child support award to include the payment of college expenses. This modification action must be filed before the child reaches the age of majority (19 in Alabama) or the action will be waived forever. If post-majority college support is an issue, refer to the earlier section discussing college support under the divorce agreement.

Most divorce experts can calculate the projected new child support payment from the gross monthly income figures for both parents as well as any day care and health insurance expenses. But there are other considerations when you seek increased support. A noncustodial parent may attempt to go after custody when the child support modification action is filed. This type of defensive action is usually apparent to the court as an effort to avoid paying higher child support, but it can create problems for the custodial parent who is seeking an increase in child support. Furthermore, if the custodial parent has had less than exemplary conduct since the divorce, he or she may not want to file for increased child support and risk custody coming into question. If the custodial parent is living with a friend of the opposite sex, for example, and this activity is brought to the attention of the trial court, the custodial parent may not only lose on the child support modification, but may also lose custody of the child as well.

Both parents have a duty to support their children. If the noncustodial parent gets a significant pay raise, an increase in child support is appropriate. Your children deserve to enjoy a lifestyle as close as possible to what they would have enjoyed if their parents remained together. However, if the noncustodial parent pays expenses beyond his child support obligation, you may not want to risk losing the extra payments to your children for a slight increase in child support. Use common sense borne out of the facts and circumstances surrounding each particular case when determining your course of action. If this could potentially be an issue in your case, sit down with your attorney and discuss the proposed new child support payment and the costs associated with achieving such a payment. As we've said before, don't spend thousands of dollars in fees and costs to win hundreds of dollars in support payments.

Visitation Modifications

After the heat of divorce has cooled, many parents alter visitation between themselves. Informal modifications are common, but they aren't enforceable by law. Most parents find that as their children get older, they and the kids need a little flexibility. This cooperation is recommended, as long as you feel okay about the changes. It is difficult and expensive, though, to get such changes mandated by the courts.

Quite often, those changes mean that a noncustodial parent gets more time with the children. For instance, a teenage child may want to take a long trip with that parent, or spend an entire summer with the noncustodial grandparents. Each request should be carefully considered by the custodial parent, keeping in mind the needs of the child, the ability of the other parent to accept this responsibility, and how the changes may affect your future rights.

The noncustodial parent should not begin to believe that each time he or she makes such a request, the other parent has to go along with it. The custodial parent still is in charge, and does not have to grant any variations to the agreed-upon visitation schedule.

These modifications, like all others, are very expensive to achieve if you have to go to court. Remember that your children will get older and their circumstances will change. If you and your spouse remain flexible, you can avoid a lot of heartache down the road.

Alimony Modifications

As stated earlier, certain forms of alimony may be modified in the future. Periodic alimony can be modified if there is a change of circumstances in the future. The burden of proving a modification to the decree is on the party seeking the change. Both the payor spouse and the recipient spouse can seek a modification of alimony. If the payor spouse's income has decreased significantly, this spouse may be able to request a decrease in the alimony payments. At the same time, if the needs of the recipient spouse have increased, that spouse may be able to request an increase in alimony. Another alimony modification involves requesting an extension of the time period of the alimony payments.

The law is specific in this area, and the court has held that a party who voluntarily quits his job may not necessarily be awarded a reduction in alimony, depending on the particular circumstances. However, a party who loses his job through no fault of his own, and who suffers a decrease in income, may be entitled to a modification in alimony. When one of the parties relies on the speculation of future events, such as a job change, a petition to modify is likely to be denied as being premature. If a modification is an issue in your case, meet with your attorney to determine whether a modification is possible in your situation.

When two people decide to get a divorce, it isn't a sign that they "don't understand" one another, but a sign that they have, at last, begun to.

Helen Rowland

CHAPTER TWENTY-SEVEN

Best Advice: Do It Right the First Time

DIVORCE IS A MIXED BAG of complex issues. If you remember anything from this book, it should be that the settlement agreement or court order must address every possible issue you can imagine that may arise after the divorce. It is extremely difficult, if not impossible, to modify many provisions after a divorce agreement has been approved by the trial court. Perhaps the best rule of thumb to follow is that if you and your spouse have not been able to agree during the marriage, it is guaranteed that you will not be able to agree on very much after the marriage.

Half of the people who get divorced for the first time will remarry, a fact you may find distasteful at this critical time. When you are in the midst of a divorce, the last thing you want to consider is getting married again. But if you leave yourself with intolerable conditions, both financially and in the custody of your children, you may face an unhappy time for years to come and your ability to remarry or have any flexibility in the way you handle relationships could be compromised.

I'll always remember a young man who came to me after his divorce was final. Although the divorce was his wife's idea, he ended up giving her custody of both children and all the marital assets as well as paying exorbitant child support and alimony. He did it, he said, "Because I didn't want my kids to suffer." When I questioned the competence of his attorney, the man said, "I was intent on giving her all of that, so I didn't think I needed an attorney." Three months after the divorce was final, she moved 2,000 miles away with a man they had both considered a friend, and now he sees his children (not to mention his furniture) once a year. His only relief was the cessation of alimony, since she remarried, but that didn't ease his broken heart.

The only way to avoid such a tragedy is to consult with an expert familiar with matrimonial law in your area, before proceeding with a divorce action. Do not execute any documents without the advice and approval of an attorney. Furthermore, do not rely upon the advice of your spouse's attorney in making a determination of what is an appropriate settlement. His or her sole purpose is to protect your spouse.

Your divorce will be one of the most difficult issues you will ever face. How you handle the divorce will greatly affect the problems you incur after the divorce. Do not believe that your spouse will do what's right and nothing will go wrong.

If a divorce is inevitable, arm yourself with a talented divorce lawyer. Consult with your attorney about the actions needed to protect yourself, and get prepared to go into battle. Hopefully, you will avoid going to war. But if you are prepared to do so, you may prevent a bad situation from becoming an impossible one.

It's like a new client of mine seeking a modification told me recently: "I had no idea how much of my future would be closely related to the divorce agreement I signed years ago. If only I had been aware of all the issues that would come up and would have hired an expert at that time."

Now she understands what's necessary to obtain the successful divorce.

Appendices A - M are resources compiled by the author for use by those contemplating a divorce or currently going through one in the state of Alabama. These appendices include charts and forms as well as lists of other resources readers can use to better inform themselves about aspects of their cases. These resources were accurate and up-to-date when they were made part of this book. Neither the author nor the publisher guarantees their accuracy or usefulness, including helping you represent yourself in divorce or post-divorce litigation. Both the author and the publisher urge you to seek legal counsel and not rely on these resources for this purpose.

Appendices A-M

Appendix A	Glossary of Family Law Terms
Appendix B	Chart of Living Expenses
Appendix C	Potential Litigation Budget
Appendix D	Estimated Child Support Expenses
Appendix E	Child Support Forms
Appendix F	Schedule of Basic Child Support Amounts
Appendix G	IRS Tax Exemption Form
Appendix H	Social Security Information Request
Appendix I	Credit Report Request Letter
Appendix J	Post-Divorce Checklist
Appendix K	Divorce Recovery Groups in Alabama
Appendix L	Alabama Child Advocacy Centers
Appendix M	List of Alabama Professionals

Appendix A
Glossary of Family Law Terms

A

ACTION: A lawsuit or proceeding in a court of law.

AFFIDAVIT: A written statement under oath.

AGREEMENT: A verbal or written resolution of disputed issues.

ANSWER: The written response to a complaint, petition or motion.

ALIMONY: A payment of support provided by one spouse to the other.

ANNULMENT: The marriage is declared void, as though it never took place.

APPEAL: A legal action where the losing party requests that a higher court review the decision.

ASSET: Everything owned by you or your spouse, including property, cars, furniture, bank accounts, jewelry, life insurance policies, businesses, or retirement plans.

ATTORNEY: A person with special education and training in the field of law. Only an attorney is allowed to give you legal advice. In family law matters, you are not entitled to a court-appointed lawyer, like a public defender in a criminal case. However, legal assistance is often available for those who are unable to hire a private attorney.

B

BILLING: An accounting of hours spent on your case by the attorney, his legal assistant and others. Usually calculated monthly.

C

CHILD SUPPORT: Money paid from one parent to the other for the benefit of their dependent or minor children.

CHILD SUPPORT GUIDELINES: Guidelines that must be followed in awarding child support. There are only a few circumstances when the court can award child support higher or lower than the guidelines.

CLOSELY-HELD BUSINESS: A business that is privately owned, such as a family business.

COMPLAINANT: The one who files the suit, same as plaintiff.

CONTEMPT: Failure to follow a court order. One side can request that the court determine that the other side is in contempt and punish him or her.

CONTINGENCY FEE: When attorneys are paid on recovery of assets in a lawsuit. This is illegal in family law cases in Alabama.

CONTINUANCE: Postponement of a trial or hearing.

CONTESTED ISSUES: Any or all issues upon which the parties are unable to agree and which must be resolved by the judge at a hearing or trial.

CONTINGENT ASSET: In some jurisdictions, an asset that you may receive or get later, such as income, tax refund, accrued vacation or sick leave, a bonus, or an inheritance.

CONTINGENT LIABILITY: In some jurisdictions, a liability that you may owe later, such as payments for lawsuits, unpaid taxes, or debts that you have agreed or guaranteed to pay if someone else does not.

CORROBORATING WITNESS: A person who testifies for you and backs up your story. If you are asking the court to grant a divorce or custody of a child, you should bring to court a witness who can corroborate your grounds for divorce or a basis for having custody.

COUNTERPETITION: A written request to the court for legal action, which is filed by a respondent after being served with a petition.

CUSTODIAL: Dealing with child custody; usually denotes the parent with custody.

CUSTODY-SOLE & JOINT: Refers to the legal arrangements for whom a child will live with and how decisions about the child will be made. Generally, the parent the child does not live with will be allowed to have regular visits with the child. The standard for custody is “best interest of the child”.

D

DEFAULT: A party’s failure to answer a complaint, motion or petition.

DEFENDANT: The person the case is brought against.

DELINQUENT: Late.

DEPOSITION: Discovery in which an attorney asks questions of the opposing party under oath.

DISCOVERY: A way of getting information from the other side or other people. Examples of discovery are interrogatories (written questions) and depositions (questions which are usually in person and recorded).

DISSOLUTION: The legal end of a marriage.

DOCKET: A court's calendar of cases.

E

ENJOINED: Prohibited by the court from doing a specific act.

EQUITABLE DIVISION: The method of dividing property in a divorce used in Alabama and most other states; involves dividing property fairly, based on a number of factors.

EX PARTE: Communication with the judge by only one party. In order for a judge to speak with either party, the other party must have been properly notified and have an opportunity to be heard.

F

FILING: Giving the clerk of court your legal papers.

FILING FEE: An amount of money, set by law, that the petitioner must pay when filing a case.

FINAL HEARING: Trial in your case.

FINANCIAL AFFIDAVIT: A sworn statement that contains information regarding your income, expenses, assets, and liabilities.

FINAL JUDGMENT OF DIVORCE: A written document signed by a judge and recorded in the clerk of the circuit court's office that contains the judge's decision in your case.

FORENSIC AUDIT: An audit or appraisal of assets for the purpose of offering testimony on its value. Such an audit is often used to value businesses and real property, anything on which there is not a commonly accepted value.

G

GROUNDS FOR DIVORCE: The legal basis for a divorce; the law sets out specific reasons for a divorce to be proven before the divorce is granted.

GUARDIAN AD LITEM: A neutral person who may be appointed by the court to represent and evaluate or investigate your child's situation, and file a report with the court about what is in the best interests of children.

H

HEARING: A legal proceeding before a judge or designated officer (general master or hearing officer) on a motion.

I

INTERROGATORIES: Written questions submitted to each party in a divorce.

J

JUDGE: An official who is responsible for deciding matters on which you and the other parties in your case are unable to agree. A judge is a neutral person responsible for ensuring that your case is resolved in a fair, equitable, and legal manner.

JUDGMENT: A court's decision.

JURISDICTION: The authority of the court to hear a case.

K

L

LIABILITIES: Debts owed by you or your spouse, including mortgages, credit cards or car loans.

LUMP SUM ALIMONY: Money to be paid by one spouse to another in a limited number of payments, often a single payment.

M

MARITAL ASSET: Generally, anything that you and/or your spouse acquired or received (by gift or purchase) during the marriage. For example, something you owned before your marriage may be nonmarital.

MARITAL LIABILITY: Generally, any debt that you and/or your spouse incurred during the marriage.

MARITAL RESIDENCE: The family home.

MEDIATOR: A person trained and certified to assist parties in reaching an agreement before going to court. Mediators do not take either party's side and are not allowed to give legal advice. They are only responsible for helping the parties reach an agreement and putting that agreement into writing.

MODIFICATION: A change made by the court in an order or final judgment.

MOTION: A request made to the court, other than a petition.

MARITAL PROPERTY: Includes all property acquired during the marriage, even if it is not titled in both names, with some exceptions.

MASTER: Hears cases like a judge. A master's decision is reviewed by a judge before becoming final.

N

NO-FAULT: A type of divorce in which the divorcing parties don't need to state specific reasons for the divorce. In Alabama, no-fault divorce does not exist, although you can divorce because of irreconcilable differences.

NONCUSTODIAL: Pertaining to the parent without custody of the children.

NONMARITAL ASSET: Generally, anything owned separately by you or your spouse.

NONMARITAL LIABILITY: Generally, any debt that you or your spouse incurred before your marriage or since your separation.

NOTARY PUBLIC: A person authorized to witness signatures on court-related forms.

O

OBLIGEE: A person to whom money, such as child support or alimony, is owed.

OBLIGOR: A person who is ordered by the court to pay money, such as child support or alimony.

ORDER: A written decision signed by a judge and filed in the clerk of court's office, that contains the judge's decision on part of your case, usually on a motion.

P

PARENTING COURSE: Teaches parents how to help their children cope with divorce and other family issues.

PARTY: A person involved in a court case, either as a petitioner or respondent.

PATERNITY ACTION: A lawsuit used to determine whether a designated individual is the father of a specific child or children.

PAYOR: An employer or other person who provides income to an obligor.

PENDENTE LITE: Temporary arrangements for custody, child support, child visitation, alimony, possession of the family home, etc., until a final hearing.

PERMANENT ALIMONY: Spousal support ordered to be paid at a specified, periodic rate until modified by a court order, the death of either party, or the remarriage of the obligee, whichever occurs first.

PERSONAL SERVICE: When a summons and a copy of a petition (or other pleading) that has been filed with the court are delivered by a deputy sheriff or private process server to the other party. Personal service is required for all petitions and supplemental petitions.

PETITIONER: The person who files the legal paper that begins a court case.

PLAINTIFF: The person who starts the case.

PLEADING: A formal written statement of exactly what a party wants the court to do in a lawsuit or court action.

PRENUPTIAL AGREEMENT: Also called a "prenup," is an agreement for the division of assets if the parties should divorce.

PRIMARY RESIDENCE: The home in which the children spend most of their time.

PROCESS SERVER: Person who serves legal papers on those being sued.

PRO SE: Representing yourself in court without an attorney.

PRO SE LITIGANT: A person who appears in court without the assistance of a lawyer.

Q

QDRO: Called a Quadro, is a planned division of a retirement account.

R

RECONCILIATION: Married people, about to divorce, getting back together.

REHABILITATIVE ALIMONY: Spousal support ordered to be paid for a limited period of time to allow one of the parties an opportunity to complete a plan of education or training, according to a rehabilitative plan accepted by the court, so that he or she may better support himself or herself.

RESPONDENT: The person who is served with a petition requesting some legal action against him or her.

S

SCIENTIFIC PATERNITY TESTING: A medical test to determine who is the father of a child.

SERVICE: Providing a copy of the papers being filed to the other side.

SETTLEMENT AGREEMENT: A document that sets out agreement between the two parties when a divorce is settled.

SPOUSE: Husband or wife.

SUBPOENA: A form issued by the court requiring someone to appear in court and/or bring documents.

SUPERVISED VISITATION: A parenting arrangement under which visitation between a parent and his or her children is supervised by either a friend, family member or a supervised visitation center, usually for the protection of the children.

SUPPLEMENTAL PETITION: A petition that may be filed by either party after the judge has made a decision in a case and a final judgment or order has been entered. For example, a supplemental petition may be used to request that the court modify the previously entered final judgment or order.

T

TRIAL: The final hearing in a contested case.

U

UNCONTESTED DIVORCE: When the defendant is not going to try to stop the divorce and there are no issues for the court to decide about the children, money or property.

V

VALUE BILLING: When the amount of attorney fees is based on hourly rate and final results.

VENUE: The jurisdiction where the case is heard.

VISITATION: The time that the parent who does not have primary residence spends with the children.

W

WRIT OF SUMMONS: A form issued by the court directing a party to respond to a complaint, motion, or petition.

Appendix B
Chart of Living Expenses

EXPENSES	MONTHLY PAYMENT
FIXED EXPENSES	$
House payment	$
Insurance	$
Home	$
Automobile	$
Health	$
Life	$
Other	$
Taxes - Home	$
FLEXIBLE EXPENSES	$
Electricity	$
Gas or Oil (Heat)	$
Telephone	$
Water and Sewer	$
Cable Television	$
Pest Control	$
Yard Care	$
Household Help	$
Repair/Maintenance	$
Other	$
FOOD	$
Groceries	$
Restaurants	$
Lunches	$
TRANSPORTATION	$
Car payment	$
Gas and Oil	$
Repairs/Maintenance	$
Auto Tag and Taxes	$
CHILDREN	$
Private School, Tutors, etc.	$
Activities (Sports, Music, Scouts, etc)	$
School lunches	$
Other school costs	$
CLOTHING/PERSONAL	$
Clothes - You	$
Clothes - Children	$
Shoes	$
Accessories	$
Laundry/Dry Cleaning	$
Beauty Shop/Barber	$
Cosmetics	$
ENTERTAINMENT	$
Newspapers	$
Magazines, Books	$
Sports, Movies, etc.	$
Vacations	$
Other Entertainment	$
EDUCATION	$
Tuition	$
Textbooks, Notebooks, Binders, etc.	$
MISCELLANEOUS COSTS/EXPENSES	$
Religious Contribution	$

Chart of Living Expenses

Gifts (Birthdays, Holidays, etc.)	$
Taxes Withheld	$
Savings	$
IRA, Other Retirement	$
MEDICAL	$
Doctors	$
Dentists	$
Orthodontist	$
Optometrist	$
Medicine/Prescriptions	$
Other	$
CREDIT CARDS (Itemize with Balance Due)	Minimum Payment
	$
	$
	$
	$
	$
PERSONAL LOANS (Itemize)	$
	$
OTHER	$
	$
TOTAL EXPENSES	$
TOTAL PERSONAL NET INCOME	$
ALIMONY PAYMENTS	$
CHILD SUPPORT PAYMENTS	$
SURPLUS OR DEFICIT	$

Appendix C
Potential Litigation Budget

TASK	PROJECTED TIME LIKELY TO BE INCURRED
Meetings with Client	
Drafting Initial Pleadings in the Case	
Drafting Temporary Support Documents	
Drafting Temporary Restraining Orders	
Drafting Protection from Abuse Pleadings	
Drafting Discovery Including Interrogatories, Request for Production, Request for Admissions and Notices of Deposition	
Meetings with Client During the Pendency of the Case	
Telephone Conferences with Client During the Pendency of the Case	
Meeting with Witnesses	
Preparing for Hearings	
Preparing Client for Hearings	
Preparing for Depositions	
Preparing Client for Depositions	
Reviewing Pleadings from Opposing Party and Responding to Same	
Taking Depositions of Opposing Party	
Attending Deposition of Client	
Taking Depositions of Expert Witnesses and Preparing for Same	
Taking Depositions of Other Witnesses and Preparing for Same	
Attending Temporary Support Hearing	
Attending the Trial	
Court Reporter's Expenses	
Photocopy Expenses	
Postage Expenses	
Deposition Expenses	

Potential Litigation Budget

Private Investigator Expenses	
Long Distance Charges	
Travel Expenses	
Costs	
Reviewing Financial Records	
Reviewing Corporate Financial Records	
Meeting with Accountant Concerning Audit of Records	
Expert Witness Cost	
Costs	
Reviewing Medical Record Issues	
Preparing Subpoena's for Witnesses and Documents	
Reviewing Information Received Pursuant to Subpoena's	
Reviewing Client's Financial Information	
Reviewing Opposing Parties Financial Information	
Preparing Responses to Interrogatories and Request for Production	
Reviewing Opposing Parties Responses to Interrogatories and Request for Production	
Preparing for and Attending Trial Settings	
Preparing for the Trial	
Preparing for the next Day's Trial in the Evening	
Miscellaneous Items	
Unanticipated Issues	
Subtotal Expenses	
Subtotal Paralegal Time	
Subtotal Attorney Time	
Total	

Appendix D
Estimated Child Support Expenses

CHILD SUPPORT EXPENSES	MONTHLY PAYMENT/CHILD'S PORTION OF THE EXPENSE
FIXED EXPENSES	$
House payment	$
Insurance	$
Home	$
Automobile	$
Health Insurance	$
FLEXIBLE EXPENSES	$
Electricity	$
Gas or Oil (Heat)	$
Telephone	$
Water and Sewer	$
Cable Television	$
Pest Control	$
Yard Care	$
Repair/Maintenance	$
Other	$
FOOD	$
Groceries	$
Restaurants	$
Lunches	$
TRANSPORTATION	$
Car payment	$
Gas and Oil	$
Repairs/Maintenance	$
CHILDREN	$
Private School, Tutors, etc.	$
Activities (Sports, Music, Scouts, etc)	$
School lunches	$
Other school costs	$
CLOTHING/PERSONAL	$
Clothes - Children	$
Shoes	$
Cosmetics	$
ENTERTAINMENT	$
Sports, Movies, etc.	$
Vacations	$
Other Entertainment	$
EDUCATION	$
Tuition	$
Textbooks, Notebooks, Binders, etc.	$
MISCELLANEOUS COSTS/EXPENSES	$
Gifts (Birthdays, Holidays, etc.)	$
MEDICAL	$
Doctors	$
Dentists	$
Orthodontist	$
Optometrist	$
Medicine/Prescriptions	$
Other	$
OTHER	$
TOTAL	$

Appendix E
Child Support Forms

State of Alabama Unified Judicial System Form CS-41 Rev. 10/93	**CHILD SUPPORT OBLIGATION INCOME STATEMENT/AFFIDAVIT**	Case Number

IN THE ______________________________ COURT OF
COUNTY

Plaintiff____v. Defendant

AFFIDAVIT

I, ____, being duly sworn upon my oath, state as follows:

1. I am the ___ plaintiff ___ defendant in the above-entitled matter.
   My Social Security Number is:
2. I am _____ currently employed. My employer's name and address is:

   _____ not currently employed.
   My last employer's name and address is:

   Last position title:
   Average monthly salary last year of employment:
3. My gross monthly income includes:
   - Employment income ______________
   - Self-employment income ______________
   - Other employment-related income ______________
   - Other non-employment-related income ______________
   - Total ______________

   3.a. I incur the following amount monthly for child care ______________
   3.b. The child(ren) of the parties is/are

   _____ not covered by health insurance from me and/or my employer

   _____ covered by health insurance and I pay the Following amount for the insurance coverage
4. I understand that I will be required to maintain all income documentation used in preparing this affidavit (including my most recent income tax return) and that such documentation shall be made available as directed by the Court.
5. I understand that any intentional falsification of the information presented in this income statement/affidavit shall be deemed contempt of court.

Affiant

Sworn to and subscribed before me this
day of ________________________, _________.

Notary/Clerk/Register

State of Alabama Unified Judicial System Form CS-42 Rev. 10/93	**CHILD SUPPORT OBLIGATION INCOME STATEMENT/AFFIDAVIT**	Case Number

IN THE ______________________ **COURT OF** ______________________ **COUNTY**

__________________________________ v. __________________________________
Plaintiff **Defendant**

Children	Date of Birth	Children	Date of Birth

	Plaintiff	Defendant	Combined
1. **MONTHLY GROSS INCOME**	$	$	
a. Minus Preexisting Child Support Payment	-	-	
b. Minus Preexisting Periodic Alimony Payment	-	-	
2. **MONTHLY ADJUSTED GROSS INCOME**	$	$	$
3. **PERCENTAGE SHARE OF INCOME** (Each parent's income on Line 2 divided by the Combined Income	%	%	
4. **BASIC CHILD SUPPORT OBLIGATION** [Apply Line 2 Combined to "schedule of basic child support obligations" (Appendix to Rule 32)]			$
5. **WORK-RELATED CHILD CARE COSTS**			$
6. **HEALTH INSURANCE COSTS**			$
7. **TOTAL CHILD SUPPORT OBLIGATION** (Add lines 4, 5, and 6)			$
8. **EACH PARENT'S CHILD SUPPORT OBLIGATION** (Multiply Line 7 by Line 3)	$	$	
9. **ADJUSTMENT FOR PAYMENT OF HEALTH INSURANCE** (If obligor pays health insurance, enter amount paid in obligor's column)	$	$	
10. **RECOMMENDED CHILD SUPPORT ORDER** (Subtract Line 9 from the amount on Line 8. Leave custodial parent's column blank.)	$	$	

Comment, Calculations, or Rebuttals to Guidelines:

PREPARED BY:	**DATE:**

State of Alabama Unified Judicial System Form CS-43 Rev. 10/93	**CHILD SUPPORT OBLIGATION INCOME STATEMENT/AFFIDAVIT**	Case Number

IN THE ______________________________ **COURT OF**
COUNTY

____v.
Plaintiff **Defendant**

- Based upon the income and expenditures supplied by parties in Form CS-41, "Child Support Obligation Income Statement/Affidavit," the child support guidelines, as set out in Rule 32, Alabama Rules of Judicial Administration, have been followed and applied.

- The child support guidelines, as set out in Rule 32, Alabama Rules of Judicial Administration, have not been followed and applied because of the following reasons:

Date:______________________________	Date:______________________________
______________________________ Signature of Plaintiff	______________________________ Signature of Defendant
______________________ AOC#: Signature of Plaintiff's Attorney	______________________ AOC#: Signature of Defendant's Attorney
______________________________ Address of Plaintiff or Plaintiff's Attorney	______________________________ Address of Defendant or Defendant's Attorney
______________________________ Telephone No. of Plaintiff or Plaintiff's Attorney	______________________________ Telephone No. of Defendant or Defendant's Attorney

State of Alabama Unified Judicial System Sample Form Rev. 9/97	**INFORMATION SHEET** **(Child Support Reform Act of 1997)**	**CASE NUMBER**

IN THE CIRCUIT COURT OF JEFFERSON COUNTY, ALABAMA

______________________________________ **v.**

Plaintiff Defendant

------- Not Applicable, No child(dren) a party to or subject to this action

Information Concerning the Parties:	Information Concerning the Parties:
Plaintiff (Mother, Father, Other_______________, or Other Party (Specify) (_ ___________________)	Plaintiff (Mother, Father, Other_______________, or Other Party (Specify) (_ ___________________)
Address (including City, State and Zip Code):	Address (including City, State and Zip Code):
Telephone Number: Home (___)	Telephone Number: Home (___)
SSN:	SSN:
Race: __________________ Sex:	Race: __________________ Sex:
Place of Employment and Address (including City, State and Zip Code (if applicable)	Place of Employment and Address (including City, State and Zip Code (if applicable)
Work Telephone Number (___)	Work Telephone Number (___)

INFORMATION CONCERNING THE CHILDREN

Name	Address(es)	Sex	DOB (dd/mm/yy)	SSN

THE CHILD SUPPORT REFORM ACT OF 1997 REQUIRES THAT THE COURT MAINTAIN THE ABOVE INFORMATION IN THE RECORD FOR ALL PARTIES WHO MAY EITHER INITIATE AN ACTION OR INTERVENE IN AN EXISTING ACTION.

Completed by:____Date Completed:

Print name Daytime Phone (205) 871-9550

Appendix F
Schedule of Basic Child Support Amounts

NUMBER OF CHILDREN DUE SUPPORT

COMB. GROSS INCOME	ONE CHILD	TWO CHILDREN	THREE CHILDREN	FOUR CHILDREN	FIVE CHILDREN	SIX CHILDREN
Below 550.00 Monthly Basic Child Support Obligation Established at the Discretion of the Court						
550.00	50	51	51	52	52	53
600.00	82	83	84	85	86	87
650.00	112	113	114	115	116	118
700.00	141	142	144	145	147	148
750.00	151	172	173	175	177	179
800.00	158	201	203	205	208	210
850.00	166	230	233	235	238	240
900.00	173	259	262	265	268	271
950.00	180	279	291	294	298	301
1000.00	187	290	320	324	327	331
1050.00	194	301	350	354	357	361
1100.00	201	312	379	383	387	391
1150.00	208	323	405	413	417	422
1200.00	215	334	418	442	447	452
1250.00	222	345	432	472	477	482
1300.00	229	356	445	502	508	514
1350.00	236	367	459	518	543	549
1400.00	243	378	474	534	577	584
1450.00	251	390	488	550	599	618
1500.00	257	399	500	564	614	648
1550.00	263	409	512	577	629	672
1600.00	269	418	524	590	643	688
1650.00	275	428	536	604	658	704

1700.00	281	437	548	617	672	719
1750.00	287	447	560	631	687	735
1800.00	294	456	571	644	701	750
1850.00	300	466	583	657	716	766
1900.00	306	475	595	671	730	781
1950.00	312	485	607	684	745	797
2000.00	318	495	619	698	760	813
2050.00	325	505	632	712	775	829
2100.00	331	514	644	726	790	846
2150.00	338	524	656	740	806	862
2200.00	344	534	669	754	821	878
2250.00	350	544	681	768	836	894
2300.00	357	554	694	782	852	911
2350.00	363	563	705	795	865	925
2400.00	368	572	716	807	879	940
2450.00	374	580	727	819	893	954
2500.00	380	589	738	832	906	969
2550.00	386	598	749	844	920	983
2600.00	391	607	760	857	933	998
2650.00	397	616	771	869	947	1012
2700.00	403	625	782	882	961	1027
2750.00	409	633	793	894	974	1042
2800.00	414	642	804	907	988	1056
2850.00	420	651	815	919	1002	1071
2900.00	426	660	826	931	1015	1085
2950.00	431	669	837	944	1029	1100
3000.00	437	677	848	956	1042	1114
3050.00	443	686	859	969	1056	1129
3100.00	449	695	870	981	1070	1143
3150.00	454	704	881	994	1083	1158
3200.00	459	712	891	1005	1096	1171
3250.00	464	720	901	1016	1108	1185

3300.00	469	728	911	1028	1121	1198
3350.00	475	736	922	1039	1133	1211
3400.00	480	745	932	1050	1145	1225
3450.00	485	753	942	1062	1158	1238
3500.00	490	761	952	1073	1170	1252
3550.00	495	769	962	1085	1183	1265
3600.00	500	777	972	1096	1195	1278
3650.00	505	785	982	1107	1208	1292
3700.00	511	794	994	1120	1222	1307
3750.00	517	803	1005	1133	1236	1322
3800.00	523	813	1017	1146	1250	1337
3850.00	529	822	1028	1159	1264	1352
3900.00	534	831	1040	1172	1278	1367
3950.00	540	840	1051	1185	1293	1382
4000.00	546	849	1063	1197	1307	1397
4050.00	552	858	1074	1210	1321	1412
4100.00	558	868	1085	1223	1335	1427
4150.00	563	877	1097	1236	1349	1443
4200.00	569	886	1108	1249	1363	1458
4250.00	575	895	1120	1262	1377	1473
4300.00	581	904	1131	1275	1391	1488
4350.00	587	913	1143	1288	1405	1503
4400.00	592	923	1154	1300	1419	1518
4450.00	598	931	1159	1313	1433	1532
4500.00	604	940	1170	1325	1446	1546
4550.00	609	948	1180	1337	1458	1560
4600.00	614	956	1190	1348	1471	1573
4650.00	619	964	1200	1359	1483	1586
4700.00	624	972	1209	1370	1495	1598
4750.00	629	980	1219	1381	1507	1611
4800.00	635	987	1229	1392	1519	1624
4850.00	640	995	1239	1403	1531	1637
4900.00	645	1003	1249	1414	1543	1650

4950.00	650	1011	1258	1425	1555	1663
5000.00	655	1019	1268	1436	1567	1676
5050.00	660	1027	1278	1447	1579	1689
5100.00	665	1035	1288	1458	1591	1701
5150.00	670	1042	1298	1469	1604	1714
5200.00	675	1050	1307	1481	1616	1727
5250.00	681	1058	1317	1492	1628	1740
5300.00	686	1066	1327	1503	1640	1753
5350.00	691	1074	1337	1514	1652	1766
5400.00	696	1082	1346	1525	1664	1779
5450.00	701	1090	1356	1536	1676	1792
5500.00	706	1097	1366	1547	1688	1805
5550.00	711	1105	1376	1558	1700	1817
5600.00	716	1113	1386	1569	1712	1830
5650.00	722	1121	1395	1580	1724	1843
5700.00	727	1129	1405	1591	1737	1856
5750.00	732	1137	1415	1602	1749	1869
5800.00	737	1145	1425	1613	1761	1882
5850.00	742	1152	1435	1624	1773	1895
5900.00	747	1160	1444	1636	1785	1908
5950.00	752	1168	1454	1647	1797	1920
6000.00	757	1176	1464	1658	1809	1933
6050.00	762	1184	1474	1669	1821	1946
6100.00	768	1192	1483	1680	1833	1959
6150.00	772	1198	1497	1689	1843	1969
6200.00	775	1203	1504	1697	1851	1979
6250.00	779	1209	1511	1705	1860	1988
6300.00	783	1214	1518	1713	1869	1997
6350.00	787	1220	1526	1721	1878	2007
6400.00	790	1226	1533	1729	1886	2016
6450.00	794	1231	1540	1737	1895	2025
6500.00	798	1237	1547	1745	1904	2035
6550.00	802	1243	1554	1753	1913	2044

6600.00	805	1248	1561	1761	1922	2053
6650.00	809	1254	1568	1769	1930	2063
6700.00	813	1259	1575	1777	1939	2072
6750.00	817	1265	1582	1785	1948	2081
6800.00	820	1271	1589	1793	1957	2091
6850.00	824	1276	1597	1801	1965	2100
6900.00	828	1282	1604	1809	1974	2110
6950.00	831	1287	1611	1817	1983	2119
7000.00	835	1293	1618	1825	1992	2128
7050.00	839	1299	1625	1833	2000	2138
7100.00	843	1304	1632	1841	2009	2147
7150.00	846	1310	1639	1849	2018	2156
7200.00	850	1315	1646	1857	2027	2166
7250.00	854	1321	1653	1865	2035	2175
7300.00	857	1326	1660	1872	2043	2183
7350.00	860	1331	1666	1878	2050	2191
7400.00	862	1336	1672	1885	2057	2199
7450.00	865	1340	1678	1891	2064	2207
7500.00	868	1345	1684	1898	2072	2214
7550.00	871	1350	1690	1904	2079	2222
7600.00	874	1355	1696	1911	2086	2230
7650.00	877	1359	1702	1917	2093	2238
7700.00	879	1364	1708	1924	2100	2246
7750.00	882	1369	1714	1930	2107	2254
7800.00	885	1374	1720	1937	2114	2261
7850.00	888	1378	1726	1943	2122	2269
7900.00	891	1383	1732	1950	2129	2277
7950.00	894	1388	1738	1956	2136	2285
8000.00	896	1393	1744	1962	2143	2293
8050.00	899	1397	1750	1969	2150	2300
8100.00	902	1402	1756	1975	2157	2308
8150.00	905	1407	1762	1982	2164	2316
8200.00	908	1412	1768	1988	2171	2324

8250.00	911	1417	1774	1995	2179	2332
8300.00	914	1421	1780	2001	2186	2340
8350.00	916	1426	1785	2008	2193	2347
8400.00	919	1431	1792	2014	2200	2355
8450.00	922	1434	1797	2020	2206	2361
8500.00	924	1438	1801	2025	2212	2367
8550.00	926	1441	1806	2030	2217	2373
8600.00	929	1445	1810	2035	2222	2379
8650.00	931	1448	1815	2040	2228	2384
8700.00	933	1452	1819	2045	2233	2390
8750.00	935	1455	1823	2050	2239	2396
8800.00	938	1459	1828	2055	2244	2401
8850.00	940	1462	1832	2060	2249	2407
8900.00	942	1466	1837	2065	2255	2413
8950.00	945	1469	1841	2070	2260	2418
9000.00	947	1473	1846	2075	2266	2424
9050.00	949	1476	1850	2080	2271	2430
9100.00	951	1480	1854	2085	2276	2435
9150.00	954	1483	1859	2090	2282	2441
9200.00	956	1487	1863	2095	2287	2447
9250.00	958	1490	1868	2100	2293	2453
9300.00	961	1494	1872	2105	2298	2458
9350.00	963	1497	1876	2110	2303	2464
9400.00	965	1501	1881	2115	2309	2470
9450.00	967	1504	1885	2120	2314	2475
9500.00	970	1507	1890	2125	2320	2481
9550.00	972	1511	1894	2130	2325	2487
9600.00	974	1514	1898	2135	2330	2492
9650.00	977	1518	1903	2140	2336	2498
9700.00	979	1521	1907	2145	2341	2504
9750.00	981	1525	1912	2150	2347	2510
9800.00	983	1528	1916	2155	2352	2515
9850.00	986	1532	1921	2160	2357	2521

9900.00	988	1535	1925	2165	2363	2527
9950.00	990	1539	1929	2170	2368	2532
10000.00	992	1542	1934	2175	2374	2538

Appendix G Internal Revenue Service Tax Exemption Form

Form **8332**
(Rev. December 2000)
Department of the Treasury Internal Revenue Service

Release of Claim to Exemption for Child of Divorced or Separated Parents

▶ **Attach** to noncustodial parent's return **each year** exemption is claimed.
Caution: *Do not use this form if you were never married.*

OMB No. 1545-0915
Attachment Sequence No. **115**

Name of noncustodial parent claiming exemption | Noncustodial parent's social security number (SSN) ▶

Part I **Release of Claim to Exemption for Current Year**

I agree not to claim an exemption for ______________________
Name(s) of child (or children)

for the tax year 20____.

______________________ Signature of custodial parent releasing claim to exemption | ______ Custodial parent's SSN | ______ Date

Note: *If you choose not to claim an exemption for this child (or children) for future tax years, also complete Part II.*

Part II **Release of Claim to Exemption for Future Years** (If completed, see **Noncustodial parent** below.)

I agree not to claim an exemption for ______________________
Name(s) of child (or children)

for the tax year(s) ______________________.
(Specify. See instructions.)

______________________ Signature of custodial parent releasing claim to exemption | ______ Custodial parent's SSN | ______ Date

General Instructions

Purpose of form. If you are a **custodial parent** and you were ever married to the child's **noncustodial parent,** you may use this form to release your claim to your child's exemption. To do so, complete this form (or a similar statement containing the same information required by this form) and give it to the noncustodial parent who will claim the child's exemption. The noncustodial parent must attach this form or similar statement to his or her tax return **each year** the exemption is claimed.

You are the **custodial parent** if you had custody of the child for most of the year. You are the **noncustodial parent** if you had custody for a shorter period of time or did not have custody at all. For the definition of custody, see **Pub. 501,** Exemptions, Standard Deduction, and Filing Information.

Support test for children of divorced or separated parents. Generally, the custodial parent is treated as having provided over half of the child's support if:

- The child received over half of his or her total support for the year from one or both of the parents **and**
- The child was in the custody of one or both of the parents for more than half of the year.

Note: *Public assistance payments, such as Temporary Assistance for Needy Families (TANF), are not support provided by the parents.*

For this support test to apply, the parents must be one of the following:

- Divorced or legally separated under a decree of divorce or separate maintenance,
- Separated under a written separation agreement, **or**
- Living apart at all times during the last 6 months of the year.

Caution: *This support test does not apply to parents who never married each other.*

If the support test applies, and the other four dependency tests in your tax return instruction booklet are also met, the custodial parent can claim the child's exemption.

Exception. The custodial parent will not be treated as having provided over half of the child's support if **any** of the following apply.

- The custodial parent agrees not to claim the child's exemption by signing this form or similar statement.
- The child is treated as having received over half of his or her total support from a person under a multiple support agreement (**Form 2120,** Multiple Support Declaration).
- A pre-1985 divorce decree or written separation agreement states that the noncustodial parent can claim the child as a dependent. But the noncustodial parent must provide at least $600 for the child's support during the year. This rule does not apply if the decree or agreement was changed after 1984 to say that the noncustodial parent cannot claim the child as a dependent.

Additional information. For more details, see **Pub. 504,** Divorced or Separated Individuals.

Specific Instructions

Custodial parent. You may agree to release your claim to the child's exemption for the current tax year or for future years, or both.

- Complete **Part I** if you agree to release your claim to the child's exemption for the current tax year.
- Complete **Part II** if you agree to release your claim to the child's exemption for any or all future years. If you do, write the specific future year(s) or "all future years" in the space provided in Part II.

TIP To help ensure future support, you may not want to release your claim to the child's exemption for future years.

Noncustodial parent. Attach this form or similar statement to your tax return for **each year** you claim the child's exemption. You may claim the exemption **only** if the other four dependency tests in your tax return instruction booklet are met.

Note: *If the custodial parent released his or her claim to the child's exemption for any future year, you **must** attach a copy of this form or similar statement to your tax return for each future year that you claim the exemption. **Keep a copy for your records.***

Paperwork Reduction Act Notice. We ask for the information on this form to carry out the Internal Revenue laws of the United States. You are required to give us the information. We need it to ensure that you are complying with these laws and to allow us to figure and collect the right amount of tax.

You are not required to provide the information requested on a form that is subject to the Paperwork Reduction Act unless the form displays a valid OMB control number. Books or records relating to a form or its instructions must be retained as long as their contents may become material in the administration of any Internal Revenue law. Generally, tax returns and return information are confidential, as required by Internal Revenue Code section 6103.

The time needed to complete and file this form will vary depending on individual circumstances. The estimated average time is:

Recordkeeping	7 min.
Learning about the law or the form	5 min.
Preparing the form	7 min.
Copying, assembling, and sending the form to the IRS	14 min.

If you have comments concerning the accuracy of these time estimates or suggestions for making this form simpler, we would be happy to hear from you. You can write to the Tax Forms Committee, Western Area Distribution Center, Rancho Cordova, CA 95743-0001. **Do not** send the form to this address. Instead, see the Instructions for Form 1040 or Form 1040A.

Cat. No. 13910F   Form **8332** (Rev. 12-2000)

Appendix H
Social Security Information Request

Form Approved
OMB No. 0960-0466 ☐ SP

Request for Earnings and Benefit Estimate Statement

☐ Please check this box if you want to get your statement in Spanish instead of English.

Please print or type your answers. When you have completed the form, fold it and mail it to us. (If you prefer to send your request using the Internet, contact us at http://www.ssa.gov)

1. Name shown on your Social Security card:

First Name ____________ Middle Initial ____

Last Name Only ____________

2. Your Social Security number as shown on your card:

☐☐☐-☐☐-☐☐☐☐

3. Your date of birth (Mo.-Day-Yr.)

☐☐-☐☐-☐☐☐☐

4. Other Social Security numbers you have used:

☐☐☐-☐☐-☐☐☐☐

☐☐☐-☐☐-☐☐☐☐

5. Your sex: ☐ Male ☐ Female

For items 6 and 8 show only earnings covered by Social Security. Do NOT include wages from State, local or Federal Government employment that are NOT covered for Social Security or that are covered ONLY by Medicare.

6. Show your actual earnings (wages and/or net self-employment income) for last year and your estimated earnings for this year.

A. Last year's actual earnings: *(Dollars Only)*

$ ☐☐☐,☐☐☐.00

B. This year's estimated earnings: *(Dollars Only)*

$ ☐☐☐,☐☐☐.00

7. Show the age at which you plan to stop working.

☐☐ *(Show only one age)*

8. Below, show the average yearly amount (not your total future lifetime earnings) that you think you will earn between now and when you plan to stop working. Include performance or scheduled pay increases or bonuses, but not cost-of-living increases.

If you expect to earn significantly more or less in the future due to promotions, job changes, part-time work, or an absence from the work force, enter the amount that most closely reflects your future average yearly earnings.

If you don't expect any significant changes, show the same amount you are earning now (the amount in 6B).

Future average yearly earnings: *(Dollars Only)*

$ ☐☐☐,☐☐☐.00

9. Do you want us to send the statement:
   - To you? Enter your name and mailing address.
   - To someone else (your accountant, pension plan, etc.)? Enter your name with "c/o" and the name and address of that person or organization.

Name ____________

Street Address (Include Apt. No., P.O. Box, or Rural Route) ____________

City ____________ State ____ Zip Code ____

Notice:
I am asking for information about my own Social Security record or the record of a person I am authorized to represent. I understand that if I deliberately request information under false pretenses, I may be guilty of a Federal crime and could be fined and/or imprisoned. I authorize you to use a contractor to send the statement of earnings and benefit estimates to the person named in item 9.

▶ ____________

Please sign your name (Do Not Print)

Date ____________ (Area Code) Daytime Telephone No. ____________

Form SSA-7004-SM Internet (6-98) Destroy prior editions

SOCIAL SECURITY ADMINISTRATION

About The Privacy Act

Social Security is allowed to collect the facts on this form under Section 205 of the Social Security Act. We need them to quickly identify your record and prepare the earnings statement you asked us for. Giving us these facts is voluntary. However, without them we may not be able to give you an earnings and benefit estimate statement. Neither the Social Security Administration nor its contractor will use the information for any other purpose.

Paperwork Reduction Act Notice and Time It Takes Statement

The Paperwork Reduction Act of 1995 requires us to notify you that this information collection is in accordance with the clearance requirements of section 3507 of the Paperwork Reduction Act of 1995. We may not conduct or sponsor, and you are not required to respond to, a collection of information unless it displays a valid OMB control number. We estimate that it will take you about 5 minutes to complete this form. This includes the time it will take to read the instructions, gather the necessary facts and fill out the form.

Mailing Address

Social Security Administration
Wilkes Barre Data Operations Center
PO Box 7004
Wilkes Barre PA 18767-7004

Request for Earnings and Benefit Estimate Statement

Thank you for requesting this statement.

After you complete and return this form, we will--within 4 to 6 weeks--send you:

- a record of your earnings history and an estimate of how much you have paid in Social Security taxes, and
- estimates of benefits you (and your family) may be eligible for now and in the future.

We're pleased to furnish you with this information and we hope you'll find it useful in planning your financial future.

Social Security is more than just a program for retired people. It helps people of all ages in many ways. Whether you're young or old, male or female, single or with a family--Social Security can help you when you need it most. It can help support your family in the event of your death and pay you benefits if you become severly disabled.

If you have questions about Social Security or this form, please call our toll-free number, 1-800-772-1213.

Kenneth S. Apfel
Commissioner of Social Security

Appendix I
Credit Report Request Letter

Credit Report Request Letter

The address of local and national credit bureau reporting firms is found in the Yellow Pages.

Name
Address
City, State, Zip

Date

Credit Bureau
Address
City, State Zip

Re: [First] [Middle Initial] [Maiden] [Last]
SSN

This is to request that a copy of my entire credit history/report be mailed to me at the above address. I have enclosed a check in the amount of $_____ to cover the cost of the report and shipping.

Thank you in advance for your prompt response to my request.

Very truly yours,

[Name]

Appendix J
Post-Divorce Checklist

Checklist	Needs to be Done	Completed
Appeal Deadline: 42 days from entry of Final Judgment of Divorce		
Prepare Deeds and File		
Real Property Deeds		
Estate Documents		
Will		
Medical Directive		
Power of Attorney		
Name Change (Probate Court)		
Automobile Titles		
Automobile Insurance		
Insurance Forms		
Life Insurance Provisions - Notify Carrier of Beneficiary Change		
Health Insurance Provisions - Notify carrier and order new identification card(s)		
Bank Accounts		
Safety Deposit Box		
Tax-IRS Forms		
IRS Form 8332 (Dependency Exemption)		
Form W-4		
Retirement Accounts / IRA / Pension		
QDRO		
Income Withholding Orders		

Appendix K
Divorce Recovery Groups in Alabama

Auburn/Phoenix City

Auburn United Methodist Church
137 South Gay Street, Auburn, AL
Telephone: (334) 826-8800

First Assembly of God
3777 Highway 431 N., Phoenix City, AL
Telephone: (334) 298-9890

Birmingham

Dawson Memorial Baptist Church
1114 Oxmoor Road, Birmingham, AL 35209
Telephone (205) 871-7324

Our Lady of Sorrows
1720 Oxmoor Road, Birmingham, AL 35209
Telephone (205) 871-8121

Briarwood Presbyterian Church Counseling Center
2200 Briarwood Way, Birmingham, AL 35243
Telephone: (205) 978-2200

Hunter Street Baptist Church
2600 John Hawkins Pike, Hoover, AL 35244
Telephone: (205) 985-7295

The Church at Brook Hills
3145 Brook Highland Parkway, Birmingham, AL
Telephone: (205) 991-0507

Valleydale Baptist Church
2545 Valleydale Road, Birmingham, AL
Telephone: (205) 991-5282

Dothan

Calvary Baptist Church
901 Montezuma Avenue,Dothan, AL
Telephone: (334) 792-5159

First Baptist Church
300 W. Main Street, Dothan, Alabama
Telephone: (334) 792-5117

New Freedom Church
115 Depot Street, Webb, Alabama
Telephone: (334) 702-8234

Fort Rucker Counseling
Building 8945 7th Avenue, Fort Rucker, Alabama
Telephone: (334) 255-3692

Decatur/Florence/Muscle Shoals/Tuscumbia

New Life Christian Church
1200 Welti Road SE, Cullman, Alabama
Telephone: (256) 734-4816

Calvary Assembly of God
1413 Glenn Street, SW, Decatur, Alabama
Telephone: (256) 355-7440

Decatur Baptist Church
2527 Danville Road, Decatur, Alabama
Telephone: (256) 353-8579

Huntsville

Whitesburg Baptist Church
6806 Whitesburg Drive South, Huntsville, Alabama
Telephone: (256) 881-0952

Pulaski Pike Church of God
3912 Pulaski Pike, Huntsville, Alabama
Telephone: (256) 852-5580

Willowbrook Baptist Church
7625 Bailey Cove Road, Huntsville, Alabama
Telephone: (256) 883-5433
First Church of the Nazarene
800 East Clinton Avenue, Huntsville, Alabama
Telephone: (256) 534-5364

Mobile

Daphne United Methodist Church
2401 Main Street, Daphne, Alabama
Telephone: (251) 626-2287

First Baptist Church North Mobile
1251 Industrial Parkway, Saraland, Alabama
Telephone: (334) 679-3266

Cottage Hill Baptist Church
4255 Cottage Hill Road, Mobile, Alabama
Telephone: (334) 660-2422

Forest Hill Church of God
5508 Moffett Road, Mobile, Alabama
Telephone: (334) 342-0233

First Baptist Church
15898 Silverhill Avenue, Silverhill, Alabama
Telephone: (334) 945-5182

Dauphin Way Baptist Church
3661 Dolphin St., Mobile, Alabama
Telephone: (334) 342-3456

Christ United Methodist Church
6101 Grelot Road, Mobile, Alabama
Telephone: (334) 342-0462

Foley United Methodist Church
915 N. Pine Street, Foley, Alabama
Telephone: (334) 943-4393

Montgomery

First Baptist Church
305 S. Perry Street, Montgomery, Alabama
Telephone: (334) 834-6310

Heritage Baptist Church
1849 Perry Hill Road, Montgomery, Alabama
Telephone: (334) 279-7176

Frazer Memorial United Methodist
6000 Atlanta Highway, Montgomery, Alabama
Telephone: (334) 260-3654

First Baptist Church
210 Sixth Street North. Clanton, AL
Telephone: (205) 755-3840

Faith Temple Church of God
4520 46th Street SW, Lanett, Alabama
Telephone: (334) 576-3904

Eastern Hills Baptist Church
3604 Pleasant Ridge Road, Montgomery, Alabama
Telephone: (334) 272-0604

First United Methodist Church
2416 W. Cloverdale Park, Montgomery, Alabama
Telephone: (334) 834-8990

First United Methodist Church
3350 Edgewood Drive, Millbrook, Alabama
Telephone: (334) 285-4114

Tuscaloosa

Valley View Baptist Church
8820 Highway 69 South, Tuscaloosa, Alabama
Telephone: (205) 752-0977

First Wesleyan Church
1501 McFarland Blvd. North, Tuscaloosa, Alabama
Telephone: (205) 752-4251

First Baptist Church
721 Greensboro Avenue, Tuscaloosa, Alabama
Telephone: (205) 345-7554

Appendix L
Alabama Network of Child Advocacy Centers, Inc.

Calhoun/Cleburne Children's Center
Greg Cole, Director
2100 Leighton Avenue, Anniston, AL 36207
Telephone: (256) 238-0902
Fax: (256) 238-0902
E-mail: tcole4cac@aol.com

Care House - Bay Minette
Baldwin County Child Advocacy Center
Blakely Davis, Director
108 Blackburn Avenue/PO Box 874, Bay Minette, AL 36507
Telephone: (251) 937-2273
Fax: (251) 937-8273
E-mail: CAREHOUSE@aol.com

Bessemer Cut-Off Advocacy Center
Randy Gilmore, Director
PO Box 306, Bessemer, AL 35021-0306
Telephone: (205) 481-4155
Fax: (205) 481-4254
E-mail: bcacenter@aol.com

Prescott House
Mary Murphy, Director
PO Box 55892, Birmingham, AL 35255-9998
Telephone: (205) 930-3622
Fax: (205) 930-3625
E-mail: mary@prescotthouse.org

CAC of Cherokee County
Lori Lumsden, Director

PO Box 587, Center, AL 35960
Telephone: (256) 927-2111
Fax: (256) 927-2110
E-mail: FTCC@tds.net

Owens House
Shelby County Child Advocacy Center
Helen Rardin, Director
PO Box 1145, Columbiana, Al 35051
Telephone: (205) 669-3333
Fax: (205) 669-0364
E-mail: ohousecac@aol.com

Brook's Place - Cullman
Child Advocacy Center of Cullman, Inc.
Susan Martin, Director
PO Box 1252, Cullman, AL 35056
Telephone: (256) 739-2243
Fax: (256) 739-2428
E-mail: caccull@cneti.com

Southeast AL Child Advocacy Center
Sherryl Walker, Director
PO Box 8781, Dothan, AL 36304-0781
Telephone: (334) 671-1779
Fax: (334) 677-1767
E-mail: SWALKER@graceba.net

Northwest AL Children's Advocacy Center
Richard Davy, Director
400 West Tennessee Street/PO Box 1336, Florence, AL 35631
Telephone: (256) 760-1140
Fax: (256) 764-3164
E-mail: rhdcac@bellsouth.net

Dekalb County Child Advocacy Center
Elizabeth Wheatley, Director
PO Box 680173, Fort Payne, AL 35968-1603
Telephone: (256) 997-9700
Fax: (256) 997-9111
E-mail: dcalcac@tds.net

Butler County CAC
Kathy Smyth, Director
PO Box 1020, Greenville, AL 36037
Telephone: (334) 382-8584
Fax: (334) 383-9485
E-mail: safeharbor@alaweb.com

Child Advocacy Center of Marshall County
Thompson House
Leslie Marshall, Director
825 Gunter Avenue, Guntersville, AL 35976
Telephone: (256) 582-8492
Fax: (256) 582-8457
E-mail: marshall@localaccess.net

National Children's Advocacy Center
Connie Carnes, Director
200 West Side Square, Suite 700, Huntsville, AL 35801
Telephone: (256) 533-0531, ext 350
Fax: (256) 534-6883
E-mail: ccarnes@ncac-hsv.org

Tri-County Children's Advocacy Center
Timothy Birt, Director
18045 US Highway 431, LaFayette, AL 36862
Telephone: (334) 864-2303
Fax: (334) 864-2356
E-mail: tri-co-cac@mail.com

Mobile Child Advocacy Center
Patrick Guyton, Director
1351 Springhill Avenue, Mobile, AL 36604
Telephone: (251) 432-1101
Fax: (251) 432-0330
E-mail: pguyton@cacmobile.org

Child Protect, Inc.
The Montgomery Children's Advocacy Center
Jannah Bailey, Director
4111 Wall Street, Montgomery, AL 36106
Telephone: (334) 262-1220
Fax: (334) 262-2252
E-mail: bailey@childprotect.org

Alabama Network of CACs (State Office)
Terry Davis, State Coordinator
PO Box 2167, Montgomery, AL 36102-2167
Telephone: (334) 834-3468
Fax: (334) 834-3469
E-mail: tdavissc@aol.com

Blount County Children's Center, Inc.
Jerry Renno, Director
106 First Avenue West/PO Box 906, Oneonta, AL 35121
Telephone: (205) 274-7226
Fax: (205) 274-9226
E-mail: BCCC@otelco.net

Child Advocacy Center of East AL, Inc.
Emilyn Gipson, Director
1810 Corporate Drive, Opelika, AL 36801
Telephone: (334) 705-0770
Fax: (334) 705-0741

St. Clair Children's Advocacy Center
Pamela Hendrick-Kelly, Director
18200 Alabama Highway 174, Pell City, AL 35125
Telephone: (205) 338-8847
Fax: (205) 338-1979
E-mail: sccac@pell.net

Russell County Child Advocacy Center
Vertrina Grubbs, Director
1011 S. Railroad Street, Phenix City, AL 36867
Telephone: (334) 297-4962
Fax: (334) 297-4794
E-mail: vgrubbscac@mindspring.com

Palmer Place
Amanda Thomas
307 S. Court Street, Talladega, AL 35160
Telephone: (256) 315-2662
Fax: (256) 315-2792
E-mail: palmerplace1@aol.com

The Tuscaloosa Children's Center, Inc.
Alesia Cook, Director
520 Martin Luther King, Jr. Blvd, Tuscaloosa, AL 35403
Telephone: (205) 752-7711
Fax: (205) 345-7297
E-mail: tcc@dbtech.net

West Alabama Children's Advocacy Center
Paul Young, Director
PO Box 685, Vernon, AL 35592
Telephone: (205) 695-8100
Fax: (205) 695-8100
E-mail: wacac@tombigbee.net

Appendix M
List of Alabama Professionals

This appendix is a list of professionals with experience helping Alabama residents work through the problems of divorce. This list is not all-inclusive. There are many more professionals in the state who perform these services. This list is merely a starting point for divorcing people wishing to solve problems unique to their situations. Neither the author nor the publisher guarantee the services of those included.

Alabama Accountants

Kenneth C. Dewitt, CPA, CFA
Dewitt & Dyer, LLC
521 Energy Center Blvd. Suite 1501, Northpoint, AL 35472
Telephone: 205-345-9898

J. Timothy Downard, CPA
Haynes, Downard, Andra, & Jones, LLP
2 North 20th Street, Suite 550, Birmingham, AL 35203
Telephone: 205-254-3380

Raiford G. "Ray" Dyer, Jr., CPA, MTA
Dewitt & Dyer, LLC
521 Energy Center Blvd. Suite 1501, Northpoint, AL 35472
Telephone: 205-345-9898

Paul Fields, Jr., CPA
Wilson, Price, Barranco, Blakenship & Billingsly, PC
3815 Interstate Court, Montgomery, AL 36109
Telephone: 334-271-2200

Alabama Accountants Continued ...

Bryan Finison, MBA, AVA
Dewitt & Dyer, LLC
521 Energy Center Blvd. Suite 1501, Northpoint, AL 35472
Telephone: 205-345-9898

G. Alan Hartley, CPA
Morrison & Smith, LLP
1809 University Blvd., Tuscaloosa, AL 35401
Telephone: 205-349-2424

George A. Henry, III, CPA, CVA
Henry & Alm, PC
120 Southside Square, Huntsville, AL 35801
Telephone: 256-539-9641

Mike Jackson, CPA
Jackson, Howard, and Whatley
729 Chestnut Street, Birmingham, AL 35216
Telephone: 205-822-2352

William D. Smith, CPA
Morrison & Smith, LLP
1809 University Blvd., Tuscaloosa, AL 35401
Telephone: 205-349-2424

William B. Stapp, CPA
Stapp & Stapp, PC
618 Alabama Avenue, Selma, AL 36701
Telephone: 334-875-9577

John West, CPA
Donaldson, Holman & West, PC
3595 Grandview Parkway, Suite 100, Birmingham, AL 35243
Telephone: 205-278-0001

Randy Whirley, CPA
Whirley & Associates
1 Perimeter Park South, Suite 100, Birmingham, AL 35243
Telephone: 205-970-6034

Alabama Counselors

Kimberly Ackerson, PhD
1027 23rd Street South, Birmingham, Al 35205
Telephone: 205-324-8499

Alabama Baptist Children's Counseling Center
PO Box 19792, Birmingham, AL 35219
Telephone: 205-982-1162

Alabama Psychiatric Services
7618 Memorial Parkway South, Huntsville, AL 35802
Telephone: 256-882-7703

Linda Alverson-Eiland, PhD
2068 Valleydale Rd Ste 2, Birmingham, AL 35244
Telephone: 205-403-0955

Bonnie L. Atkinson, PhD
444 North Cedar St, Florence, AL
Telephone: 256-767-6139

Sue Trant Bargeron, PhD
AL Psychotherapy & Wellness Ctr
631 Beacon Parkway West Ste 203, Birmingham, AL 35209
Telephone: 205-912-2002

Missy Beard
Covenant Counseling Center
2204 Lakeshore Drive, Birmingham Al 35209
Telephone: 205-879-7500

Alabama Counselors Continued ...

Sharon Bell, LPC
505 South Perry St, Montgomery, AL 36104
Telephone: 334-265-1009

Barbara Bernstein, MA, LLC
2112 11th Avenue South, Suite 515, Birmingham, AL 35205
Telephone: 205-322-1818

Tammy Bond
Covenant Counseling Center
2204 Lakeshore Drive, Birmingham Al 35209
Telephone: 205-879-7500

Bill Braden
Brookwood Forest Elementary School
3701 Brookwood Road, Mountain Brook, AL 35223
Telephone: 205-877-8349

Adam Calvert
I Found Hope Counseling Center
3145 Brook Highland Parkway, Birmingham AL 35242
Telephone: 205-408-7181

Jim Cotton
Cotton, McInturff & Associates, PC
2305 Arlington Avenue, Birmingham, AL 35205
Telephone: 205-933-9276

Kelly Cousins, LPC
New Life Clinic
200 Office Park Drive, Birmingham, AL 35223
Telephone: 205-879-9964

Covenant Counseling & Education Center
2204 Lakeshore Drive, Suite 214, Birmingham, AL 35209
Telephone: 205-879-7500

Daphne T. Dickerson
Alabama Counseling Institute
3928 Montclair Road Ste 219, Birmingham, AL 35213
Telephone: 205-871-1713

Rebecca I. Dossett, PhD, MFT
Cotton, McInturff & Associates, PC
2305 Arlington Avenue, Birmingham, AL 35205
Telephone: 205-933-9276

Miriam Drummonds
Cotton, McInturff & Associates, PC
2305 Arlington Avenue, Birmingham, AL 35205
Telephone: 205-933-9276

Kyle Echols, MD
1903 Oxmoor Road, Birmingham, AL 35209
Telephone: 205-879-2700

Marian Elledge, MA
Adult & Child Development Professionals
Cotton, McInturff & Associates, PC
2305 Arlington Avenue, Birmingham, AL 35205
Telephone: 205-933-9276

Glenda R. Elliot, PhD
Adult & Child Development Professionals
Cotton, McInturff & Associates, PC
2305 Arlington Avenue, Birmingham, AL 35205
Telephone: 205-933-9276

Dr. Laura English
New Life Clinic
200 Office Park Drive, Birmingham, AL 35223
Telephone: 205-879-9964

Alabama Counselors Continued ...

Dr. Lenora Ennix
Harbor Counseling Center
2000 Providence Park, Suite 100, Birmingham, AL 35242-4632
Telephone: 205-981-2990

Family Services Center
2227 Drake Av, SW, Huntsville, AL 35805
Telephone: 256-551-1610

Denise Fournet, PhD
1600 7th Ave So, Birmingham, AL 35233
Telephone: 205-877-3558

Alice H. Frederick, PhD
131 Fairhope Avenue, Fairhope, AL 36532
Telephone: 205-928-5656

Vivian Friedman, PhD
UAB Semolian Clinic
1700 7th Avenue S., Birmingham, AL 35294
Telephone: 205-934-4912

Dr. Sharon Gotlieb
AL Psychotherapy & Wellness Ctr
631 Beacon Parkway West Ste 203, Birmingham, AL 35209
Telephone: 205-912-2001

Anna Green
I Found Hope Counseling Center
3145 Brook Highland Parkway, Birmingham AL 35242
Telephone: 205-408-7181

Fletcher Hamilton Ph D
1 Independence Plaza, Birmingham, AL 35209
Telephone: 205-871-0031

Andrea Hampton
I Found Hope Counseling Center
3145 Brook Highland Parkway, Birmingham AL 35242
Telephone: 205-408-7181

Melinda Higginbotham
New Life Clinic
200 Office Park Drive, Birmingham, AL 35223
Telephone: 205-879-9964

Dr. Trey Hill
I Found Hope Counseling Center
3145 Brook Highland Parkway, Birmingham AL 35242
Telephone: 205-408-7181

Beth Jacobs, PhD
Shealy Holt & Jacobs
1613 21st Street South, Birmingham, AL 35205
Telephone: 205-933-7849

Steven Kaczor, PsyD, JD
Grayson & Associates
#2 Riverchase Ridge, Suite 100, Birmingham, AL 35244
Telephone: 205-444-0420

Karl Kirkland, PhD
Kirkland, King & Renfro
1520 Mulberry Street, Montgomery, AL 36106
Telephone: 334-269-1106

Luther E. Kramer, M Div LIP, LMFT
North Alabama Center for Pastoral Counseling
219 Grove Avenue, Huntsville, AL 35801
Telephone: 256-534-2560

Alabama Counselors Continued ...

Dr. Paul LaRussa
350 Canyon Park Drive, Pelham, AL 35124
Telephone: 205-664-8721

Robin McInturff
Cotton, McInturff & Associates, PC
2305 Arlington Avenue, Birmingham, AL 35205
Telephone: 205-933-9276

Dr. Noble McKnight
Harbor Counseling Center
2000 Providence Park, Suite 100, Birmingham AL 35242-4632
Telephone: 205-981-2990

Mark Means
I Found Hope Counseling Center
3145 Brook Highland Parkway, Birmingham AL 35242
Telephone: 205-408-7181

Dr. H Dixon Mitchell
Canterbury Counseling Center
350 Overbrook Rd, Mountain Brook, AL 35213
Telephone: 205-879-0202

New Life Clinic
200 Office Park Drive, Birmingham, AL 35223
Telephone: 205-879-9964

Hank Payne
I Found Hope Counseling Center
3145 Brook Highland Parkway, Birmingham AL 35242
Telephone: 205-408-7181

Sue Pearson
I Found Hope Counseling Center
3145 Brook Highland Parkway, Birmingham AL 35242
Telephone: 205-408-7181

Robert M Pitts Jr, PsyD
Grayson & Associates
2200 Lakeshore Drive, Suite 150, Birmingham, AL 35209
Telephone: 205-871-6926

Dr. Frankie Preston
525 Fountain Road, Huntsville, Al 35801
Telephone: 256-534-7107

Guy Renfro, PhD
Kirkland, King & Renfro
1520 Mulberry Street, Montgomery, AL 36106
Telephone: 334-269-1106

Beebe Roberts, MA
Cotton, McInturff & Associates, PC
2305 Arlington Avenue, Birmingham, AL 35205
Telephone: 205-933-9276

Harriet Schaffer, MA
Family Therapy Associates
813 Shades Creek Parkway, Homewood, AL 35209
Telephone: 205-870-5955

Dr. Travis Tindale
Covenant House
3001 Cahaba Heights Road, Birmingham, AL 35243
Telephone: 205-967-3575

Alabama Counselors Continued ...

Keith D. Thompson, MA
Cotton, McInturff & Associates, PC
2305 Arlington Avenue, Birmingham, AL 35205
Telephone: 205-933-9276

Dr. Karen Turnbow
AL Psychotherapy & Wellness Center
630 Beacon Parkway West Ste 203, Birmingham, AL 35209
Telephone: 205-912-2000

Sharon Turner PhD
Family Therapy Associates
813 Shades Creek Parkway, Homewood, AL 35209
Telephone: 205-870-5955

Kenneth J. Wade, PhD
Cotton, McInturff & Associates, PC
2305 Arlington Avenue, Birmingham, AL 35205
Telephone: 205-933-9276

Leah Waller
I Found Hope Counseling Center
3145 Brook Highland Parkway, Birmingham AL 35242
Telephone: 205-408-7181

Nancy J. Wasson, PhD
Fox Run Counseling Services
3411 Casey's Crossing, Birmingham, AL 35215
Telephone: 205-680-4311

Bob Wendorf
4213 Dolly Ridge Road, Birmingham AL 35243
Telephone: 205-970-5509

Don Wendorf, PhD
4213 Dolly Ridge Road, Birmingham AL 35243
Telephone: 205-970-5509

Dr. Dale Wisely
Vaughan Psychiatric
1600 7th Avenue South, Suite 500, Birmingham AL 35223
Telephone: 205-939-9193

Ron Yount
I Found Hope Counseling Center
3145 Brook Highland Parkway, Birmingham AL 35242
Telephone: 205-408-7181

Alabama Estate Planners

Charles Barton Adcox
Phelps, Jenkins, Gibson & Fowler, L.L.P.
P.O. Box 020848, Tuscaloosa, AL 35402
Telephone: 205-345-5100

Bill Bryant
Feld, Hyde, Wertheimer & Bryant, PC
2000 Southbridge Parkway, Suite 500,Birmingham AL 35209
Telephone: 205-802-7575

John J. Crowley, Jr.
Coale, Dukes, Kirkpatrick & Crowley
2610 B Dauphin Street, Suite 101, Mobile, AL 36606
Telephone: 334-471-2625

C. Fred Daniels
Cabiness, Johnston, Gardner, Dumas & O'Neal
2001 Park Place North, Birmingham, AL 35203
Telephone: 205-716-5232

Alabama Estate Planners Continued ...

L.B. Feld
Feld, Hyde, Wertheimer & Bryant, PC
2000 Southbridge Parkway, Suite 500, Birmingham AL 35209
Telephone: 205-802-7575

Richard Mark Kirkpatrick
Coale, Dukes, Kirkpatrick & Crowley
2610 B Dauphin Street, Suite 101, Mobile, AL 36606
Telephone: 251-471-2625

Melinda Matthews
Sirote & Permutt
2311 Highland Avenue S., Suite 500, Birmingham, AL 35205
Telephone: 205-930-5101

Kay Wilburn
Feld, Hyde, Wertheimer & Bryant, PC
2000 Southbridge Parkway, Suite 500, Birmingham AL 35209
Telephone: 205-802-7575

Alabama Financial Planners

Beverly Barry
NBC Securities
1927 1st Ave N., Birmingham AL 35203
Telephone: 205-421-2235

James W. Baxter
Berchot, Baxter & Associates LLP
3500 Colonnade Parkway, Suite 150, Birmingham, AL 35243
Telephone:

Randy Bennett
1200 Winner Avenue SW, Huntsville, AL 35805
Telephone: 256-536-9580

Greg Canfield
The Canfield Agency
701 Montgomery Highway, Birmingham, AL 35216
Telephone: 205-822-5477

Patrick Dunn, C.L.U.
One Office Park, Suite 307
PO Box 91627, Mobile, AL 36691
Telephone: 334-344-1480

Steven Gill
3500 Colonade Parkway, Birmingham, AL 35243
Telephone: 205-970-5286

Charles D. Haines, LLC
600 University Place, Suite 501, Birmingham, AL 35209
Telephone: 205-871-3334

Wayne Harris
First Financial Group
200 Office Park Drive, Birmingham AL 35223
Telephone: 205-803-3333

Robert Ireland
Merrill Lynch
420 North 20th Street, Birmingham, AL 35203
Telephone: 205-326-9543

Zach Ivey
First Financial Group
200 Office Park Drive, Birmingham AL 35223
Telephone: 205-803-3333

Alabama Financial Planners Continued ...

Michael R. Jones
PO Drawer 2107, Decatur, AL 35602
Telephone: 256-353-8224
Karen King
603 E Second Street, Sheffield, AL 35660
Telephone: 256-383-6711

Robert R. Lott, CLU, CHFC
3500 Colonade Parkway, Suite 130, Birmingham, AL 35242
Telephone: 205-380-2600

GayNell Palmisano, CRIA
Heritage Planning Group P.C.
1420 Government Street, Mobile, AL 36604
Telephone: 251-876-8011

Dawn Peeples, Financial Representative
2990 Highway 280, Suite 210, Birmingham, AL 35223
Telephone: 205-271-7016

Mary Weir
Horizons Planning
3900 Montclair Road, Suite 280, Birmingham, AL 35213
Telephone: 205-871-7743

Stewart Welch, III, CFP
The Welch Group, LLC
3940 Montclair Road, 5th Floor, Birmingham, AL 35213
Telephone: 205-879-5001

Alabama Mediators

Lee Borden
3280 Morgan Drive, Birmingham, AL 35216
Telephone: 205-979-6960

Robin Burrell
2125 Morris Avenue, Birmingham, AL 35203
Telephone: 205-250-8459
Doug Key
Key, Greer, Frawley, Key, Harrison & Simpson
2163 Highway 31 South, Suite 102, Pelham, AL 35124
Telephone: 205-987-2211

Sam Kok
2121 Highland Avenue, Birmingham, AL 35205
Telephone: 205-939-0033

Alabama Mortgage Specialists

Susan Adams
A.M. Robbins Mortgage, Inc.
600 Luckie Drive, Suite 400, Birmingham, AL 35223
Telephone: 205-871-1905

Regina D. Clement
Diversified Mortgage
3512 Old Montgomery Highway, Birmingham, AL 35209
Telephone: 205-879-5626

Rob Coats
Coats & Company
2000-B Southbridge Parkway, Suite 150, Birmingham, AL 35209
Telephone: 205-871-5600

Alabama Mortgage Specialists Continued ...

Chris Robbins
First Commercial Bank
800 Shades Creek Parkway, Birmingham, AL 35209
Telephone: 205-868-4744

Clay Wilkinson
Magellan Mortgage Services
2004 G Poole Drive, Huntsville, AL 35810
Telephone: 256-859-9696

Dolan Williams
Gulf States Mortgage
741 Volare Drive, Birmingham, AL 35244
Telephone: 205-988-4567

Alabama Private Investigators

Jack Atkins
Divorce Investigations
PO Box 360283, Birmingham, AL 35236
Telephone: 205-991-7575

Clinton Clay, LCSW
3322 Century Office Center, Huntsville, AL 35810
Telephone: 256-881-0884